HARPERS
FERRY

HARPERS FERRY

Ray Jones

PELICAN PUBLISHING COMPANY
Gretna 1992

The word "Pelican" and the depiction of a pelican are trademarks of
Pelican Publishing Company, Inc., and are registered in the U.S.
Patent and Trademark Office.

Library of Congress Cataloging-in-Publication Data

Jones, Ray, 1948-
    Harpers Ferry / Ray Jones.
       p.   cm.
    ISBN 0-88289-832-9
    1. Harpers Ferry (W. Va.)—History. I. Title.
F249.H2J66   1992
975.4'99—dc20   91-36015
                                        CIP

Cover photo by Bruce Roberts

*All photographs courtesy of Harpers Ferry National Historical Park unless
otherwise credited.*

Manufactured in the United States of America

Published by Pelican Publishing Company, Inc.
1101 Monroe Street, Gretna, Louisiana 70053

*To Robert Harper, Joseph Barry, Thomas Jefferson,
and Grace McEntee*

Contents

HARPERS FERRY

Prologue

This is the story of an American town and of the floods of history that have swept over it.

High Water

At four o'clock in the afternoon on Friday, September 30, 1870, an urgent dispatch arrived at the railroad telegraph office in Harpers Ferry. Storms had dumped heavy rains on the Blue Ridge Mountains, and the Shenandoah River had broken out of its banks. The rampaging river had already flooded the town of Front Royal, about fifty miles to the south, and the citizens of Harpers Ferry were advised to expect the worst. The warning came too late. The telegraph had barely stopped clicking when the river flushed an angry red and began to growl.

That is not its usual character. On most days the Shenandoah slinks past Harpers Ferry as if it thinks the town is asleep and is afraid to wake anybody up. Rivers are temperamental, however, and none changes moods more quickly than the Shenandoah. Just before it meets the Potomac, the valley of the Shenandoah narrows dramatically, forcing the river through a vise of rock. Flood waters trapped behind the closed-in valley walls have no place to go but up; as a consequence, a couple of rainy days can quickly become a major event.

11

This sketch depicts the great Shenandoah flood of 1870, the same one that carried eccentric inventor John Wernwag down the river on the roof of his house.

Although calamity is its most frequent visitor, Harpers Ferry has survived for more than two centuries. Above, an 1889 Potomac rampage turns the village into a lake.

Not surprisingly, the people of Harpers Ferry have seen a lot of high water. Usually, in the face of a flood, the town's disaster-hardened residents stand their ground. They lug their furniture up the steps and spend the night upstairs. That is exactly what most of them intended to do this time. The waters would recede just as they always had in the past, and the patient refugees would trudge back down the stairs, sweep out the mud and grime, and go on with their lives as before. Or so they thought, but they had never before seen a flood like this one.

With a single, irresistible surge the river smashed the bridges linking the main part of Harpers Ferry with low-lying Virginius Island. Families marooned on the island barely had time to scramble upstairs. From the supposed safety of their upper rooms they watched the water climb steadily after them and listened to the fearsome barking of fallen limbs and debris slamming against the sides of their houses. Soon, the flood was nipping at their heels, driving them out onto their roofs.

Townsfolk who had managed to reach high ground kept an all-night vigil on the rocks above the river. Although tormented by the cries of their trapped friends and neighbors, they could do nothing to help. They could only watch in horror as one by one the Virginius Island homes collapsed and were carried away by the swirling water.

The last of the homes fell at ten o'clock the next morning. The doomed house belonged to an aging tinker named John Wernwag, an eccentric thought by many to be a mechanical genius. A quiet man of very retiring habits, he never ventured outside his home, which doubled as a machine shop. Some said the only occasion likely to draw him out of his house was his own funeral.

Wernwag had waited out more floods than anyone could count, and nobody doubted that he was still in the house when it went down. Nor did anyone who witnessed the calamity doubt that he had been crushed by the collapsing

A logjam of debris washed into Shenandoah Street by the 1924 flood.

B & O gondolas loaded with stone help hold the Potomac railroad bridge in place during a record flood in 1936.

High water on Market Street during an August 1955 flood.
(Courtesy HFNHP, photo by James P. Gallagher)

walls. There was no sign of him in the debris littering the water's churning surface.

The roof of the house remained intact, and, being shoved along by the flood, it crashed into a tree and broke in half. No sooner had this happened than the old man was seen nimbly scrambling up through the wreckage. He had no chance to reach shore, but he did find momentary safety on a piece of the shattered roof, a floating remnant of his former home. As he was hurried downstream toward the rocky junction of the Potomac and the Shenandoah, Wernwag raised a hand as if to wave good-bye to his old friends. It was his seventy-sixth birthday.

That night a Baltimore and Ohio Railroad train steamed into Harpers Ferry from the east. It chugged slowly across an old trestle bridge, which had survived the flood only because it spanned the Potomac and not the Shenandoah. The sight of the train raised the spirits of the town's battered residents by reminding them that they still had a link with the outside world. Most heartening of all was the sight of a familiar figure clambering down the steps of a passenger car. Wernwag's friends and lifelong acquaintances had been sure he was dead. Now they were astonished to see him standing before them at the B & O station, bruised, muddied, but still very much alive. He had just completed one of the most remarkable round trips in the town's history, having traveled the six miles to Brunswick, Maryland, on the roof of his house and then back again by train. Wernwag had survived yet another flood.

Time Is a River

Like John Wernwag, Harpers Ferry itself has survived many floods. The town has always been, and remains today, firmly in the grip of nature, its nearest neighbors being the Shenandoah and the Potomac, two of America's most unruly rivers. When either of them goes on a rampage, the town pays a dreadful price. On a number of occasions—in 1870, 1877, 1889, 1896, 1924, 1936, 1942 and as recently as

1972, after Hurricane Agnes—it was all but destroyed. High-water marks can be seen far up on the walls of the buildings along Shenandoah and Potomac Streets.

No town in America can lay claim to more tales of disaster than Harpers Ferry. In addition to the floods that have turned its streets into spillways for overflowing rivers, it has been devastated by fire and plague, invaded and held hostage by terrorists, assaulted by infantry, overrun by cavalry, and shelled from three sides by cannon. It has been hit hard by depression, prohibition, and plain, old-fashioned bad luck.

The accumulation of disasters at Harpers Ferry has been so great that while most of the rest of the nation has grown up and its numbers increased geometrically, Harpers Ferry has shrunk. Today its population hovers around 370. Residents are fond of saying that their community has one person for every day in the year with a few extra to fill out the total in case anybody gets washed down the river.

The town was once much larger. During its prime, Harpers Ferry was an industrial center with a government-supported weapons industry and dozens of other productive enterprises. It stood astride a heavily traveled pathway to the west, at a breach carved by the Potomac in an otherwise solid wall of mountains. The Baltimore and Ohio Railroad and the Chesapeake and Ohio Canal channeled the nation's commerce through this gate, and Harpers Ferry was more than happy to serve as tollkeeper. By 1859, the year John Brown made his famous—or infamous—raid, the place had upwards of 3,000 residents, which is 2,999 more than it had in 1747, the year it was founded by Robert Harper.

A lonely and impoverished carpenter, Harper had been driven to the road by financial misfortune. When he laid eyes on the scenic junction of the Shenandoah and Potomac, he decided to set aside both his wanderings and his carpentry skills and settle down to the business of fetching travelers across the rivers in a canoe. It was Harper who first exhibited the stoic tenacity that has always characterized residents of the town he founded. On more than one occasion he was forced to stand by helplessly and watch as houses he had built with his own hands were swallowed up by floods. Each time Harper lost a house to the rivers, the stubborn ferryman pulled out his carpenter's tools and built another. Over the years, others built houses nearby and Mr. Harper's ferry became a town. When the federal government established a musket factory there, at the insistence of George Washington, the town began to hum.

With its strategic location, resources, and industry, Harpers Ferry might have grown into a major city much like Pittsburgh, another town founded in the eighteenth century at a junction of rivers. But Pittsburgh's rivers were kinder to her and so was history. The steel city was never forced to endure a bloody raid by terrorists, never subjected to repeated attacks by two mighty and hostile armies who, like the Potomac and Shenandoah, did not regard Harpers Ferry as friendly territory.

The American Civil War began, not at Fort Sumter, but at Harpers Ferry. The first shot of the war was fired by one of John Brown's raiders as he crossed into town over a wagon bridge spanning the Potomac—ironically, the bullet struck and killed a black man. Afterwards, like salmon returning to their native stream, soldiers came to Harpers Ferry again and again to die and to spawn more battles. The town never recovered from the beating it took in the war. That is why Harpers Ferry is known, not as a manufacturing center, but as the place where John Brown (the abolitionist commando and terrorist) confronted Robert E. Lee (the U.S. Army colonel and soon-to-be Confederate general).

Today, part of Harpers Ferry has been set aside as a national historical park. Hundreds of thousands of Americans visit the park each year searching for their past. For those who look closely and pause to consider, the park offers a better understanding of the John Brown Raid, the Civil War, and of a lot more American history besides. But just beyond the park boundary, visitors will see some important monuments that can't be found in a museum: houses, gardens, children, and a school. There's still a town at Harpers Ferry. Although it has no shopping centers, freeways, or skyscrapers, although a few dozen votes are enough to elect its mayor, although battered and muddied, Harpers Ferry remains very much alive.

1

Shenandoah Falls at Mr. Harper's Ferry

A Hole in the Wall

The Potomac and Shenandoah Rivers meet at a sharp cleft in the long, jutting abutment of the Blue Ridge. The early, westward bound settlers who passed through this deep mountain notch knew it simply as "The Hole." That's a rather unpoetic name for the place where the muskets that saved Fort McHenry were crafted, where the first shot of the Civil War was fired and where the outcome of that particularly American tragedy may have been decided, where the American industrial revolution was born, where a liberating social revolution (the N.A.A.C.P.) was launched, and where American presidents (Washington, Jefferson, Madison, Adams, Pierce, and Lincoln, to name a few) crossed paths again and again.

The name "Harpers Ferry" serves the town and its remarkable history only a little better than "The Hole." Still the place itself is dramatic even if its name is not. Thomas Jefferson certainly thought so. After journeying there to gather material for his travel book, *Notes on Virginia*, Jefferson described the view from Harpers Ferry in seemingly contradictory terms. "Placid and delightful," he called it, and also "wild and tremendous." He said he thought the view was "worth a trip across the Atlantic." These would be among the most controversial words Jefferson ever set down on paper, even more so than his assertion in the Declaration of Independence "that all men are created equal" (an enormous philosophical leap in the eighteenth century and one, alas, still not universally accepted today). Although his fellow travel writers panned him mercilessly for praising the scenery at Harpers Ferry, most of today's visitors side with Jefferson.

The grand vista that inspired Jefferson was created through the interaction of stone and water. The Potomac River rises in the Allegheny Mountains, a saw-toothed range of mountains streaked with coal and minerals. Rushing headlong out of what once was western Virginia and now is the state of West Virginia, it pushes past cliffs and boulders and cuts down through a shield of 500-million-year-old rocks until reaching the formidable natural barrier of the Blue Ridge. There it is strengthened by its one notable tributary, the Shenandoah, which flows out of a green and gracious valley reaching more than a hundred miles down into the agricultural heartland of the Old South.

At their junction, the two rivers share their finest, most powerful moment. Joining forces at the point where Maryland, Virginia, and West Virginia touch, they rush against the 1,200-feet-high Blue Ridge, break it open, and spill eastward toward the city of Washington where the combined rivers lose themselves in the watery abundance of the Chesapeake Bay. But at The Hole, their distinct characters are still very much in evidence: the robust Potomac forcing its way down from the northwest, the genteel Shenandoah cutting in from the south.

In coming together, the rivers sharpen a narrow outcropping of ageless granite. A scattering of antique buildings clings like dried blood to this gray stone blade, their bricks stained dark red by flood, fire, and time. This is Harpers Ferry.

Leopards and Lions

Harpers Ferry has stood on its eastward-pointing finger

of rock for more than two centuries—since Robert Harper's arrival in 1747—but the river junction itself has been known far longer. In 1669, a German-born adventurer named John Lederer set out to explore the dark reaches beyond the recently settled Virginia tidelands. Lederer said he struggled to the crest of a ridge of mountains and peered over into a broad valley on the other side. He may have been the first European to look down on the meeting place of the Shenandoah and Potomac. But there are doubts about what he saw.

Unable to push farther into the mountains, Lederer returned to the colonial capital at Jamestown. At the time, the royal governor of Virginia was Sir William Berkeley, an intolerant man who often railed against the evils of free schools and printing presses. Berkeley had hired the explorer to find a water route to the Indian Sea. There was, of course, no such passage, but the governor was as dogmatic in his notions about geography as he was on the subject of education. When Lederer returned without having found a passage, Berkeley dumped him unceremoniously out of the colony.

Once in Maryland, safely out of Berkeley's reach, Lederer did the one thing most certain to gall his former employer—he published a book describing his travels. And what a strange and wonderful book it was. Lederer tells of the splendid view he had of the Atlantic Ocean from the summit of the Blue Ridge (not likely), the marvelous pearls worn by the Indians he met (less likely), and the fierce leopards and lions he encountered (impossible). Lederer's map places mountains where there are no mountains, rivers where there are no rivers. Historians give Lederer more credit for his imagination than for his discoveries.

A conservative and unadventurous bunch, the Tidewater Virginians were highly skeptical of Lederer's claims but unwilling to go and see for themselves. Almost half a century passed before another expedition ventured into the blue-tinged mountains on Virginia's western horizon. This one was led by a governor, Alexander Spotswood, who set off in

1716 wearing a green velvet riding suit and sporting a sweeping plume in his hat. Spotswood apparently considered the journey something of an extended fox hunt since he took with him about a dozen properly attired Virginia gentlemen and a wagonload of wine and liquor. According to a diary kept by one of the governor's tipsy companions, the explorers were sustained by ample supplies of "red wine, Irish usquebaugh [whiskey], brandy shrub, two sorts of rum, champagne, canary, cherry punch, water cider . . . and so forth." Spotswood's party reached the banks of the Shenandoah, drank a toast to the English king, and turned back. None of the governor's men reported sightings of leopards and lions, but heaven knows what other fantastic animals they saw.

A House in The Hole

Not long after the Spotswood expedition staggered back to Jamestown, young Robert Harper began his own adventure in America by emigrating from Oxford, England, to Philadelphia. For twenty-five years he enjoyed moderate success as an architect, carpenter, and millwright, but things turned sour for Harper when he built a church for a congregation of Pennsylvania Anglicans. For some reason the worshippers would not or could not pay him for his work. Financially ruined by this disaster, the dejected Harper turned his back on the "City of Brotherly Love." Thinking he might have better fortune with a different denomination in another colony, the ever-trusting builder accepted an offer to build a meetinghouse for a group of Quakers in northern Virginia.

By 1746, the year Harper set out for Virginia, the settled part of America still extended only a few miles from the coast. Leaving his wife behind in the safety of Philadelphia, he trekked across a wilderness of cold rivers and giant trees broken only rarely by recently cleared farmsteads and rough cabins inhabited by hardy huntsmen. Harper had intended to cross over the Potomac and into Virginia at a ford near the mouth of Antietam Creek. Then, at a lonely inn deep in the forests of Maryland, he met a German settler named Hoffman who suggested a better route. Hoffman told Harper about a ferry located in an impressive gorge, which some unromantic pioneer had named "The Hole." Harper could cross the Potomac there and keep his feet and his tools dry. When Harper arrived at The Hole a day or so later, the ferry turned out to be nothing more than a simple canoe, its paddles manned by Peter Stevens, a stout backwoodsman, and Gutterman Tom, his Indian companion. Still, the canoe served its purpose well enough, and it gave Harper an idea.

About a year later Harper drove the last pegs into the Quaker meetinghouse, put out his hand, and collected his due from the scrupulous Society of Friends. With gold coins jingling in his pocket, Harper believed his luck had finally turned. He was determined to invest the money, but he was in no mood to press his luck by building any more churches. Having decided to give up carpentry, he had a very different line of business in mind—the ferry business. Returning to The Hole, he paid Stevens thirteen British guineas for the canoe, a corn patch, and a crude log cabin. Then he sent for his wife.

On the morning before she arrived, Harper heard a ferry customer call out to him from the north bank of the Potomac. "Hallo, the boat," called the traveler.

"Oh yea," came the ferryman's reply.

Harper took his canoe across the river and, while exchanging pleasantries with his customer, was given the happy news that Mrs. Harper was approaching. The traveler had seen her a few miles back struggling towards The Hole in a wagon filled with household goods.

"I don't think they will ever get here . . . over the road I came on," said the traveler. "God knows that no horses ever hauled a load over such rocks before."

Eventually, with the help of Harper's German friend Hoffman, Mrs. Harper did manage to reach The Hole. No

A wagon and mule team cross the Shenandoah on a rope-drawn ferry about 1876.

doubt, she was given a solicitous welcome by her husband for whom she had abandoned a civilized existence in Philadelphia. It is easy to imagine Mr. Harper pointing with enthusiasm to the mountains and rivers, and arguing the merits of the place. It is just as easy to imagine Mrs. Harper shaking her head at the sight of the rustic cabin that was now her home and questioning the benevolence of the "Good Lord" for landing her in The Hole.

"I know how I got here," said Mrs. Harper, "but heaven knows how I shall ever get out." As fate determined, many years later she would make her exit by means of a ladder.

On many occasions, Mr. Harper, too, must have questioned the wisdom of his decision to settle at this particular river junction. He certainly had his doubts on the day he discovered that Peter Stevens and Gutterman Tom had been squatters. The true owner of the property was Lord Fairfax, who held legal title to all the "northern neck of Virginia." The luckless Harper had to buy the land all over again from Fairfax, this time for fifty guineas. Harper grumbled but paid up, figuring that, after all, he'd made a good investment. In the quick-running rivers he saw strength—power to turn millstones and someday, perhaps, to set factory wheels spinning.

He was right enough about the power of the rivers. In 1748, only a year after he moved in, the Shenandoah flooded and carried away his little cabin. Harper built another. At harvest time, six years later, a second inundation again drove the carpenter-turned-ferryman to high ground, this one bringing on its crest a tide of bobbing pumpkins washed from the gardens of Indian farmers upstream.

Fortunately for Harper, he never sold his hammers, chisels, saws and adzes. After the "Pumpkin Flood," he threw up yet another house and set to work on a gristmill beside the Shenandoah as well as a sturdy ferryboat to replace the canoe. He also made plans for a stone residence to be built well up on a spine of rocks beyond the reach of the often angry rivers. But good masons being hard to find on the frontier, construction of the house was delayed for decades. Shortly after the first stones were finally laid in 1775, Harper's masons and most of the other skilled workmen in Virginia hurried off to help George Washington fight the British. It took Harper seven years to complete the structure—about the same length of time it took Washington to defeat the redcoats—and he died in 1782 without ever having lived in it.

It is said Harper amassed a fortune with his ferry and through his many and various dealings at The Hole, but no one knows for sure. When he died, his aging wife promptly buried the family valuables to keep them safe from marauding soldiers of the Crown and freebooting revolutionaries. Three days later, the old woman slipped and fell from a ladder while working on a wall of the still unfinished Harper residence. Her bones were brittle, and she soon died from injuries received in the fall—without having told anyone where she had hidden the treasure. Some say the value of the so-called Harper fortune has been vastly exaggerated and that it probably never amounted to much more than three hundred dollars. Nonetheless, the search for the "treasure" has attracted astrologers, fortunetellers, diviners, and no few archaeologists. Despite their best efforts, the loot, if it exists at all, remains buried somewhere beneath the streets of the town.

Harper may or may not have died a rich man, but at The Hole he wrote his name with indelible ink on the ledger of history. The community that grew up around his ferry was at first known as Shenandoah Falls. But travelers persistently referred to it as "Shenandoah Falls at Mr. Harper's Ferry." In time this rather awkward name was understandably shortened to Harpers Ferry—no one knows what happened to the apostrophe.

After Harper's death, the stone house became an inn and tavern. Among its earliest guests were the men destined to become the third, and fourth presidents of the United States.

2

Jefferson and Madison at "The Hole"

Worth a Trip Across the Atlantic

As a young man, Thomas Jefferson became addicted to travel. To help him remember all the places he visited, he made a habit of jotting down his observations in pencil on loose sheets of paper. Since he was also addicted to the natural sciences—in his day, these were less fields of serious research than they were the playthings of country gentlemen—he analyzed everything he saw.

For Jefferson, logic was a religion. Wherever he went, he scoured his surroundings for evidence of an ordered universe, and, of course, he always found some. To Jefferson's mind, his native Virginia was an especially orderly place, and over the years, his notes on the geology, botany, zoology, even archeology of the colony piled up into a small mountain.

Towards the end of the Revolutionary War, a French diplomat asked Jefferson to sort through his notes and draw some of his less technical observations into a small volume describing the scenery of Virginia, perhaps as a guide for foreign travelers. Flattered and ever anxious to please a Frenchman, Jefferson set about the task with his usual awesome thoroughness. Not satisfied to simply edit what he had already written, he planned a series of special field trips to study his subjects firsthand.

*One of the earliest published depictions of Harpers Ferry and
the passage of the Potomac through the Blue Ridge, this
scene appeared in a magazine about 1854.*

*According to legend, this is the rock where Jefferson stood to
view the twin gorges of the Potomac and Shenandoah rivers.*
(Photo courtesy of Bruce Roberts)

Jefferson arrived at Harpers Ferry in October of 1783, took a room at the recently completed Harper Tavern, and mounted the steep hill behind the building. Not far from the grassy plot where Robert Harper had been buried only a few months earlier, he discovered a peculiar balanced rock, part of an exposed outcropping offering an expansive view. Others might have been content merely to enjoy the grand scenery, but not Jefferson. Instead, the future president busied himself with feverish note taking. He was sure he could see evidence "of a war between rivers and mountains, which must have shaken the earth itself to its centre." Methodically, he recounted the events that led to this battle between forces of nature.

Never one to leave a rung off an intellectual ladder, Jefferson carried his reconstruction all the way back to the beginning of time: "that this earth has been created in time, that the mountains were formed first, that the rivers began to flow afterwards, that in this place particularly they have been dammed up by the Blue Ridge of Mountains, and have formed an ocean which filled the whole valley; that continuing to rise they have at last broken over at this spot, and have torn the mountain down from its summit to its base."

The lines dance to a familiar rhythm. It seems that we have heard them before, and no wonder. In 1776 Jefferson used similar language to construct a rather famous argument: "We hold these truths to be self-evident, that all men are created equal, that they are endowed by their Creator with certain unalienable rights, that among these . . . That . . . That . . . That these United Colonies are, and of Right ought to be Free and Independent States. . . ."

Jefferson's passage on Harpers Ferry concludes only a little less dramatically. "This scene," he wrote, "is worth a voyage across the Atlantic.

Had old Governor Berkeley—that enemy of public education and printing presses—lived a century later, it might have pleased him to learn that Jefferson could not get his *Notes on Virginia* published in America. Presses were so few in the newly independent states and printing costs so high that the work had to wait until the author himself had made a voyage across the Atlantic—sailing in the opposite direction. In 1784, while serving as U.S. ambassador to France, he ordered two hundred copies from a press in Paris.

Once he had the books, Jefferson handed them out only to a few close friends and associates. He had raised some controversial questions about slavery, and the politician in him feared the stir they would cause in America. However, there soon appeared an unauthorized and poorly translated version in French. Horrified by the mutilation of his prose, Jefferson hurried the original to a London book dealer for general publication.

After the release of *Notes on Virginia*, Jefferson received little criticism for his comments on slavery—it was a flammable issue but not yet ready for the match. Instead, he drew fire from travel writers for having "amazingly exaggerated" his description of the view from Harpers Ferry. Decades later, after retiring from the presidency and politics, Jefferson was still defending himself against the charge. In a letter written at Monticello in 1809, he angrily conceded that "the same scene may excite very different sensations in different spectators according to their different sensibilities." He, on the other hand, was sure enough of what he had seen at Harpers Ferry.

Naturally, Jefferson was unwilling to entrust his memory to the uncertain prose skills of another writer. So, well in advance of his death in 1826, he took up a pen and wrote his own epitaph. Jefferson's tombstone mentions that he was author of *Notes on Virginia*, but it says nothing about his two terms as president of the United States.

Madison Gets Wet

It was probably at Jefferson's suggestion that James Madison, his dear friend and political ally, visited Harpers Ferry in 1786. In a letter to Jefferson, the tactful Madison was quick to praise the scenery thereabouts as "magnificent," but then admitted that he had not gotten a very good look at it.

"I viewed it, however, under great disadvantages," said Madison. "The air was so thick that distant objects were not visible at all, and near ones not distinctly so. We ascended the mountain, also, at a wrong place, fatigued ourselves much in traversing it before we gained the right position, were threatened the whole time with a thunderstorm, and finally overtaken by it."

Although drenched and exhausted, Madison later stood beside the Potomac and watched in fascination while fifty sweating and splashing laborers struggled to dredge the river's stony channel. These men worked for the Potomac Company, which aimed to open the river to navigation as far inland as Cumberland, Maryland, more than two hundred miles from the sea.

3

Mr. Washington's "Favorite Object"

Washington Crosses the Potomac

The father and president of the Potomac Company was the same man whose portrait now appears on the one-dollar bill. George Washington had a material turn of mind. Unlike Jefferson or Madison, it might never have occurred to him to climb a steep hill merely to study nature or take in an extraordinary view. When Washington looked down into the blue water of the Potomac, he saw an investment—a big one.

Washington saw western Virginia for the first time at age sixteen, when he went there to survey the Shenandoah Valley for Lord Fairfax. The year was 1748, and the journey carried the teenaged surveyor to The Hole where a certain carpenter from Pennsylvania had recently settled and had his cabin swept away by flood.

When George Washington and Robert Harper met, perhaps they discussed the great potential of the rivers—here was the power needed to drive mill wheels and here was a highway to carry goods and produce from the west. But Washington himself was less impressed by the rivers than by the land he surveyed to the west of Mr. Harper's Ferry. It was dirt cheap but likely to balloon in value, especially if the Potomac could be developed as a highway to the interior of the country. The youthful Washington was not yet a wealthy man, but he wanted to be one, and following the French and Indian War, he and his family started buying up western acreage. Having married a rich widow named Martha Dandridge, he had plenty of money to throw into the venture.

Washington had a good head for business. When the Continental Congress made him general of the revolutionary army, he insisted on serving without pay, asking only that he be reimbursed for his expenses. During the six-year war against the British, the general managed to log hundreds of thousands of dollars on this open-ended expense account. At the war's end, an amazed but grateful Congress had no choice but to bite their lips and pay up.

The Revolution made Washington the most powerful and celebrated man in America—he was also rapidly becoming one of the wealthiest—but under the Articles of Confederation the nation had no presidency to give him. Resigning from the army, he turned his attention to what some of his friends called "the favorite object of his heart"—the Potomac. With help from Tobias Lear and George Gilpin, two downstream businessmen who, like Washington, stood to profit mightily from opening the river to wider commerce, he formed the Potomac Company.

By 1785, Potomac Company crews were pulling snags and boulders out of the river, but the work did not progress smoothly. Formidable obstacles were encountered, particularly at Harpers Ferry where the Potomac churns over a series of stair-step ledges. After many delays and much expense, company engineers finally managed to breach the ledges and forge an artificial channel. River barges could pass through, but they careened down the channel like logs in a flume. Only a few boatmen were willing to risk the wild ride. Not surprisingly, this portion of the new Potomac "highway" attracted little traffic.

Meanwhile, the Potomac project was causing a stir downstream. Washington was not the only one who saw riches in the west, and since the Potomac formed the border between Maryland and Virginia, officials from the two states raised a loud squabble over who should control navigation on the river. Determined to see that nothing should hinder the flow of profits, Washington arranged a parlay to settle the dispute. The conference on "navigation of interstate waterways" was held in 1786 at Mount Vernon in rooms decorated with pine paneling, which had been painted dark to look like mahogany. Just as the paneling had done, the conference underwent a remarkable transformation. The delegates started out haggling over barge rates and canal lock tolls but ended up proposing the overthrow of the United States government. Actually, it wasn't much of a government in the first place; under the Articles, the American economy had reached such a sad state that a farmer needed roughly a pound of Continental currency to buy a pound of bread from a village baker. Even if the Potomac did make someone a lot of money, it would be worthless. So there were few complaints when the Mount Vernon gathering was followed about a year later by a constitutional convention in Philadelphia. Like a team of engineers designing locks to float America past a set of dangerous rapids, the conventioneers gave the country distinct legislative, judicial, and executive branches of government.

One result was that, in 1793, the president of the Potomac Company also became president of the United States. To Washington's thinking, the two offices were quite complementary, and the nation's first chief executive invited Congress to build a new federal capitol at the edge of a Potomac swamp within carriage-riding distance of his Mount Vernon plantation. Later, when the War Department needed an arms factory, he had a place in mind for that also— Harpers Ferry, a few dozen miles up the Potomac from the infant city of Washington, D.C.

A Steamboat at Harper's Ferry

George Washington was well acquainted with Harpers

Ferry. Not only had he surveyed the area as a teenager, he had visited the town as recently as 1788 to spur on the failing efforts of the Potomac Company to make the river navigable. The project had been placed in the hands of James Rumsey, an inventor and engineer of extraordinary talent. However, it is possible that Rumsey was not totally committed to the task. Unlike Washington, the Potomac was never the "favorite object of his heart." For Rumsey that place was filled by the steamboat he had tinkered with for nearly a decade.

Some years earlier, Washington himself had seen a model of the boat and was so impressed that he made Rumsey the chief engineer of the Potomac Company. In 1786, Rumsey brought a larger, though unfinished, demonstration model to Harpers Ferry—still known to many then as Shenandoah Falls—so that he could wrestle with his boat and Washington's river simultaneously. About fifty feet in length, the steamboat was assembled one piece at a time with parts made to Rumsey's specifications in Baltimore and Frederick or at the nearby Antietam Iron Works. No doubt, many of those who saw Rumsey working on the strange, hissing contraption shook their heads and spat on the ground in disbelief. How could he possibly expect to power a boat with boiling water?

By late in 1786, Rumsey had pistons and gears in place and was planning to silence the doubting Thomases with a public demonstration. Then, as so often happens at Harpers Ferry, the rivers changed his plans. A flood tore the steamboat from its moorings and smashed it against the rock ledges in the Potomac.

Another year passed before Rumsey could repair the damage, but by December 3, 1787, he was ready for his demonstration. With a roaring fire under its boiler, the steam engine in the boat's belly sputtered and wheezed. There was "a great bubbling up of the water behind" the vessel, and to the amazement of a throng of spectators, Rumsey's boat began to move upstream against the strong Potomac current. Among those on hand to witness this spectacle was Gen. Horatio Gates, the Revolutionary War hero. The old general could not contain his excitement. "My God!" he shouted. "She moves!"

To the delight of everyone watching, the boat steamed up and down the river between Shepherdstown and the Potomac ledges just above Harpers Ferry. Boys ran along the shore trying to keep pace with the vessel, not a difficult task since it chugged along at only about three miles per hour.

In spite of the boat's unimpressive speed, Rumsey's accomplishment attracted wide acclaim. It drew attention from the likes of Benjamin Franklin, who founded a "Rumseian Society" in Philadelphia. Franklin served as president of the group and helped raise the money to send Rumsey to England. There the inventor hoped to build a larger steamboat, demonstrate it, and win acceptance for his idea among European scientists and shipbuilders.

Naturally, Rumsey made the trip to England in the only form of ocean transportation available at that time—a sailing ship. It may have rankled the inventor to note that the winds of the Gulf Stream pushed the ship along at much faster speeds than his steamboat had managed on its first run near Harpers Ferry. Nonetheless, Rumsey remained convinced that steam power was the wave of the future for watercraft. In fact, he was so sure of himself that he shared his thoughts, perhaps, a bit too freely. Among those fascinated by Rumsey's concept was a young American then traveling in Europe. The traveler's name was Robert Fulton, and it is believed that he met Rumsey in London in 1792.

Before the end of that year, Rumsey had nearly completed his new steamboat—this one a hundred feet in length. Although seriously ill, he was almost ready to take the vessel for a test run on the fabled Thames River. Then tragedy struck as Rumsey's hopes and dreams piled up and sank on the shoals of his own death from what apparently were natural causes. The inventor was buried in England and largely forgotten. No one is sure of what happened to his model. Years later, Robert Fulton launched the *Clermont*, the first commercially practical steamboat. In keeping with an uncharitable tradition almost as old as the inventive mind of humankind, Fulton cheerfully claimed full credit for the idea.

The Perfect Spot for an Armory

With Rumsey gone, the effort to make the Potomac fully navigable bogged down and was eventually abandoned. Meanwhile, George Washington was distracted by the duties of public office, but the president had not lost interest in his river. Far from it.

To defend its hard-won independence the nation required a strong militia, and that made necessary a reliable arms factory or armory. With his old friends Lear and Gilpin cheering him on, Washington cajoled a doubtful Congress for money to build an armory on the Potomac. In fact, he knew just the place for it—Harpers Ferry.

Maybe President Washington had forgotten about the flood that had wrecked Rumsey's first steamboat and the many other violent "freshets" that had roared through The Hole since his first trip to the area—not long after a major flood in 1748. In any case, the susceptibility of the river junction to floods did nothing to dampen his enthusiasm for Harpers Ferry as the location for a strategic, federally funded industry. When advisors suggested alternate locations, Washington's finger came down heavily on the map of Virginia. "This spot," he said, indicating the junction of the Potomac and Shenandoah, "affords every advantage."

Washington's dealings with engineers were not always so friendly as his late relationship with poor Rumsey. Hired by the War Department to find a likely site for an armory, military engineer Stephen Rochfontaine turned in a report that did not even mention Harpers Ferry. The president was not at all pleased.

Pressed for an explanation, Rochfontaine pointed out that the town had "no ground on which convenient buildings could be placed" and, worse, "no water works would be safe there" because of the likelihood of floods. But Washington would hear none of this. He demanded the engineer be sent back to Harpers Ferry with orders to revise his report. Rather than do this, Rochfontaine resigned.

The War Department had been opposed to the Harpers Ferry armory from the first. Secretary of War Henry Knox suggested the government construct an armory at Springfield, Massachusetts, instead. Surprisingly, Knox's chief agreed to the proposal. Perhaps, Washington believed this would clear away opposition to construction of a larger, more important arms facility at Harpers Ferry. It did not.

Having secured a Federal plum for Massachusetts, Knox retired at the early age of forty-four. This left the War Department in the hands of Timothy Pickering, a skilled bureaucrat very much opposed to building a second armory at Harpers Ferry. It was Pickering who had commissioned Rochfontaine's report. When this backfired on him, the new secretary of war turned to the more effective tactic of delay. Under pressure from the president, Pickering bought 125 acres from Harper heirs John and Sarah Wager for a little more than $7,000. But by the time Washington passed the presidency to fellow Federalist John Adams in 1797, not a single brick had been laid for the armory workshops.

After another year elapsed with no action, the exasperated Washington wrote a letter to James McHenry, secretary of war under President Adams. Could it be, asked Washington, "that a place of this importance . . . which has already cost the United States several thousand dollars has passed unnoticed . . . ?" He praised Harpers Ferry as "a place of immense strength . . . unaccessible by an enemy."

McHenry had learned from his predecessors. He delayed.

Then, late in 1798, war with France loomed. The French, who had been so helpful during the War of Independence, were caught up in their own revolution, which had begun ten years earlier and seemed likely to go on forever. They were also at war with the British and were angry with the Americans for remaining neutral. It was a dangerous world. McHenry ordered work to commence on the United States Armory at Harpers Ferry. Meanwhile, Adams placed Washington, now sixty-seven years old, in command of the American military, and the aging general promptly dispatched three regiments, roughly one-quarter of his entire force, to the junction of the Shenandoah and Potomac. He was determined to keep his investment safe.

The Politics of Building an Armory

When armory superintendent Joseph Perkin arrived at the river fork in the fall of 1798, he brought with him fifteen expert gunsmiths ready to set to work turning out muskets. However, Harpers Ferry was not ready for *them*. The village had no place for them to live, let alone to ply their craft.

The Harpers Ferry of 1798 was hardly more than a cluster of rough-hewn wood or stone houses. It had a small sawmill, several stables, and a few sheds, but no schools, churches, or hotels. A single country store carried on a meager cash-and-barter trade with local farmers.

Perkin was a master gunsmith, but he had no engineering experience. Secretary of War McHenry knew he could not rely on the superintendent to oversee construction of the armory buildings and the canal that would bring fast-flowing water to power the gun factory's trip-hammers. Instead, this work was left in the hands of paymaster John Mackey, a man of feverish ambition and political zeal. A staunch Federalist, Mackey handed out jobs and graded salaries in strict accordance with party loyalties.

The American political pot was at a fast boil. The sharply contrasting attitudes of Jefferson and Washington toward life and government had hardened into a pair of bitterly opposed factions. The Federalists had enjoyed twelve years of dominant influence under Washington and Adams. Jefferson's Republicans (also known as Democrats) were about to wrest power for themselves, but only after one of the meanest political wars in American history.

Dating from the early 1800s, this rendering may show armory buildings.

The famous architect Benjamin Henry Latrobe had expressed an interest in designing the arms factory, but McHenry rejected his bid because he was "known to be in the closest sympathy with all the Virginia democrats." Mackey considered this a great victory since he hated anyone with even the slightest taint of association with Jefferson. Besides, he felt perfectly capable of designing the armory workshops himself.

Not until the spring of 1799 had Mackey gathered from rural Maryland and Virginia a large enough force of brick-burners, bricklayers, and carpenters for work to begin. Once he had laborers, Mackey pushed them hard to get the project back on schedule. By pressing his men incessantly, he was able to see the main armory structures standing along the Potomac within six months. In triumph, Mackey reported to the War Department: "The Smith shop and Factory are finished. The Arsenal [a warehouse for storing completed weapons] is built. . . . All, even my numerous Democratic Enemies, agree that the Buildings are elegant."

During the years that followed, Superintendent Perkin would be reminded over and again that this construction had been done too fast. Walls cracked, roofs sagged, and timbers gave way. But by the time the buildings began to self-destruct, Mackey's political arrogance had long since proved his undoing.

The armory needed a canal to draw power from the Potomac for its water-driven machinery, and Mackey could not build this in a slapdash manner as he had the armory buildings. The canal would have to stand up to the river's frequent floods, and the water flowing through it would have to be carefully regulated. Rejecting suggestions that he employ a professional engineer for this task, Mackey took full responsibility for construction of the mile-long water course. In his opinion, digging the canal required "no ingenuity." Certainly, it did require a large number of men willing to toil long hours in a sweltering, mosquito-infested river bottom, and these Mackey could not find. Even the offer of a daily whiskey ration failed to attract the laborers he needed, causing Mackey to rail against the "habitual laziness of the poor."

Like Mackey, the local Federalist hardliners he hired at inflated salaries to supervise the effort understood nothing about excavating a canal. The project lagged, and this raised eyebrows at the War Department. In July of 1799, the paymaster claimed that "1/2 of the canal" was complete. About a week later, he told McHenry that "about 1/3 of the canal is dug." When winter brought digging to a stop, he reported that "3/4 of the whole is yet to be puddled." Rather than lengthening, the canal seemed to be shrinking.

However, it was Mackey's personality and his treatment of employees that finally brought him down. As early as February of 1799, his policy of supplying armorers with low-quality, often rotten food sparked a seven-day strike. More trouble erupted when he fired William Small, a worker popular with local residents. The paymaster saw the uproar as a Jeffersonian conspiracy aimed solely at him.

Mackey fretted in a letter to a friend: "The levity of Small made him a suitable Engine in the hands of Democrats for embarrassing me. . . . He then circulated reports that I had beaten a pregnant woman to abortion, shot a negro Man, attempted to ravish his own wife, Mrs. Small, and filched a poor man somewhere in the Western Counties of all his money. . . . Never was a Man more universally hated than I am. . . ."

Mackey was right enough about his popularity. Soon, the citizens of the town, Superintendent Perkin, his armory workers, officials at the War Department, and even George Washington were howling for him to resign. On a cold winter's night Mackey packed his belongings and slipped out of town under cover of darkness. He was not seen in Harpers Ferry again.

Rolling Down Jefferson's Rock

Factional strife did not leave the river junction with

Mackey. The troops Washington dispatched to Harpers Ferry under Gen. Charles Pinkney brought a heavy dose of it with them. Some taunted the Federalists while others baited the Republicans (the forerunners of today's Democrats), their bickering often deteriorating into fist fights and even duels.

The odd, balanced rock from which Jefferson once viewed the "passage of the Potomac" figured prominently in one of these squabbles. A century afterward, lifelong Harpers Ferry resident and chronicler Joseph Barry (we shall hear more of him later) would describe the incident this way: "a certain Captain Henry in General Pinkney's army is said to have taken his company one day to Jefferson's Rock and ordered them to overthrow the favorite seat of Jefferson, his political enemy. They succeeded in detaching a large boulder from the top which rolled down hill to Shenandoah Street, where it lay for many years, a monument to stupid bigotry. This action was the occasion for a challenge to mortal combat for Captain Henry from an equally foolish Republican in the same corps, but the affair having come to the ears of General Pinkney, he had both of the champions arrested before a duel could come off, very much to the regret of all the sensible people of the town who expect that if the meeting were allowed to take place there would be, probably at least, one fool the less in Harpers Ferry."

George Washington might have agreed with Barry. In his farewell address to the nation, the old, worn-out revolutionary had urged his countrymen to avoid party discord, but as it would seem, to no avail. Washington caught a severe cold at Mount Vernon and passed from the scene on December 14, 1799, barely missing the arrival of a new century and a wholly different era. The death of the nation's most famous occasional soldier, part-time politician, and full-time businessman united the entire country in mourning. In little more than a year, Jefferson would unite it further, sweeping the elections of 1800, defeating Washington's Federalists, and lodging his own party in power for the next twenty-four years.

4

The Business of Making Weapons

A Shaky Beginning

For people such as Samuel Anin, politics are less important than the need to get things done. A New Jersey businessman who had been a wartime comrade-in-arms of McHenry, Anin took over as paymaster on May 1, 1800, and immediately attacked the problem of the unfinished canal. One of the first things he did was to fire the worthless supervisors who owed their appointments to Mackey's political cronyism. Next, to provide the project with a large and stable labor force, he sought help from the army. For an offer of one dollar a week and double rations, as many as a hundred of Pinkney's soldiers volunteered for service puddling and banking the canal.

Early the following year, canal water finally started pouring over the five armory mill wheels to power tilt hammers and grindstones. At last Perkin and his gunsmiths could begin making weapons. But the canal leaked, and the craftsmen worked slowly. By the end of 1801, the armorers had completed only 293 muskets, and those were of an outdated design in use since the French and Indian War. These few guns seemed a meager return on the $82,231.64 the U.S. government had invested at Harpers Ferry—roughly $7,000 for land and $75,000 for construction and equipment.

47

The armory had a better year in 1802, producing 14,722 muskets. By that time, however, Pinkney's troops had long since packed up and gone home. The threat of war with France, which had led to creation of the armory, was forgotten. Of course, there would be other wars.

And a Professor of the English Language

After construction of the armory, Harpers Ferry grew slowly but steadily. Joseph Scott's geographical dictionary published in 1805 lists the town as having, in addition to government facilities, only about fifteen houses and a post office. Another published in 1810 contained this entry:

"Harpers Ferry: Though small in appearance, contains upward of 700 souls. It has a good tavern, several large stores for goods, a library, one physician, and a professor of the English language."

The Gentleman from Virginia

An epidemic of "bilious fever"—probably either yellow fever or malaria—swept into Harpers Ferry during the summer of 1806. The disease, which claimed dozens of victims, was believed at the time to have been spread by noxious vapors rising from the rivers. Abandoning homes and workbenches, armorers fled into the surrounding mountains.

One gunmaker who remained in the stricken town was Joseph Perkin, who refused to flee with his men. His bravery and determination, though admirable, did not save him from the plague. He came down with the fever in the fall and succumbed to it a few weeks before Christmas.

The War Department offered the superintendent's job to New England inventor Eli Whitney, a gunsmith by trade. Whitney was caught up in a nasty lawsuit over the rights to his famous cotton gin and could not accept. For what apparently were political reasons, the appointment then fell to William Stubblefield, a Virginia planter with no previous experience in the large-scale manufacture of arms. Legend has it that to qualify for the position Stubblefield had to

Superintendent of the Harpers Ferry Armory for two decades, gentleman farmer James Stubblefield was among the first to employ mass production techniques in the manufacture of firearms.

build a musket with his own hands starting with only basic materials. For this purpose, he locked himself in a small country workshop in Virginia and emerged about a month later with an acceptable if not handsome piece. Henry Dearborn, secretary of war under Jefferson, then offered him the job at an annual salary of $1050 plus rations.

Our Flag Was Still There

During Jefferson's first term in office, his administration remained committed to a balanced budget. Total federal expenditures ranged from $5 million to $10 million per annum (the government now spends that much in about five minutes). Outlays for the military, including those for the Harpers Ferry and Springfield armories, were cut to the bone.

Then, in 1803, Britain continued an ages-old tradition and went to war against the French, who under Napoleon had conquered most of Europe. Jefferson hoped the United States could stay neutral. By 1805, however, the British were stopping American merchant vessels on the high seas, seizing contraband cargo, and even impressing American sailors into service on warships. Suddenly, a balanced budget no longer seemed important.

Dearborn urged Stubblefield to step up production at Harpers Ferry, whatever the cost. The armory must now produce, not 14,000, but "from 15 to 20,000 muskets annually and a due proportion of Rifles, Pistols, and Swords." The new superintendent enlarged existing buildings, had several additional workshops built, and ordered construction of fifteen houses to board the new workers he hoped to recruit. All this came at a price. Armory expenses soared from about $40,000 in 1807 to more than $100,000 the following year.

Still Stubblefield could not meet the urgent demands of the War Department. With war on the horizon, public and private armories across the country snapped up the skilled gunsmiths he needed to increase production.

Under intense pressure from Secretary Dearborn, Stubblefield came up with an astonishing innovation. Unable to hire skilled armorers, he employed inexperienced men instead and set them to work on simple, repetitive tasks. Where a craftsman might have been expected to turn out a completed musket lock, now he made only one small component of the lock. Eventually, the superintendent broke the process of making a musket down into sixty separate operations, and as specialization increased, the work grew easier, faster, and cheaper.

Many years later Stubblefield would claim credit for having invented the concept of division of labor in the manufacture of firearms. In fact, he probably picked up the idea from Whitney or from the Springfield armory. But he was one of the first factory managers anywhere to use this technique of mass production.

Despite Stubblefield's breakthrough, production at Harpers Ferry never matched that of the Springfield armory. Even so, countless thousands of muskets flowed from the mouth of the Shenandoah into hands of American soldiers, sailors, and militiamen. These weapons helped repulse the 1814 British attack on Baltimore's Fort McHenry— named for the former secretary of war who, under pressure from George Washington, had ordered construction of the Harpers Ferry armory.

The muskets did not, however, prevent the British from invading the city on the Potomac that had been named for Washington. The unsympathetic redcoats burned the Capitol and White House, driving a panic-stricken James Madison westward into the wilds where he and the presidential household found themselves at the mercy of the elements. It was not the first time Madison had been caught out in a thunderstorm.

Machines, Not Gunsmiths

While America struggled frantically to prepare for the approaching War of 1812, a Yankee genius labored quietly in his workshop on the coast of Maine. He was making a new kind of rifle and, without knowing it, starting an economic revolution that has not yet ended.

Fashioning each piece by hand, John Hall created a rifle that could be loaded at the breech rather than the muzzle. To ready a muzzle-loading weapon for action a soldier had to stand, pour a charge of powder into the barrel, and then ram home the paper wadding and a lead ball with a cumbersome rod. Hall's rifle eliminated most of these steps. A soldier could reload much faster and do it from the relative safety of a crouched position. He no longer needed to stand erect, making an easy target of himself. As a bonus, the rifle also offered greater firepower and improved accuracy.

For all these very good reasons Hall expected to make a fortune by manufacturing his new rifles and selling them to the American military. Instead, he fell victim to an outrageous scam. The superintendent of patents, Dr. William Thornton, refused to issue Hall a patent on the grounds that he, Thornton, had already invented a similar rifle. Although he had neither drawings nor a working model to support his claim, Thornton maintained that he had "thought" of the invention some years earlier. Being a "reasonable" man, however, he was willing to share a patent with Hall.

The New Englander tried to fight this banditry, but he had no friends in Washington. Thornton had plenty. Seeing no other alternative, Hall finally agreed to a joint patent in May 1811. But the partnership was short-lived. Thornton wanted to peddle the patent at a high price to an established arms manufacturer such as Whitney. Hall, on the other hand, demanded exclusive right to build the rifle himself. The dispute between the two dragged on for years keeping the new weapon out of production until long after the redcoats had burned Washington and sailed for home.

Hall would have been forced into bankruptcy had he not been rescued by John C. Calhoun, the young secretary of war appointed by Pres. James Monroe. Calhoun was intrigued by the military potential of the new rifle and rightfully so. Had they been armed with Hall's breech-loaders, the American militiamen who tried in vain to defend the capital in 1814 might have driven the British back to the Chesapeake.

Determined to provide American fighting men with better weapons, Calhoun decided to take a chance on the Hall rifle. First, he bought out Thornton's interest in the patent. Next, he ordered a thousand of the breech-loaders and sent their true inventor to the national armory at Harpers Ferry to fulfill the contract. Hall would receive a royalty of one dollar for each rifle made and a salary of sixty dollars per month for serving as an armorer. Hall considered this a pauper's return on the years he had devoted to the rifle and the family fortune he had invested in it. But he had no choice. He accepted Calhoun's offer and set out for Virginia.

At Harpers Ferry, Hall faced still more vexing difficulties. Superintendent Stubblefield took an instant disliking to this outsider from the North as well as his newfangled rifle. As a consequence, the facilities given to Hall at the armory proved inadequate and the workers assigned to his project were decidedly inferior. What was worse, Hall discovered that even the most experienced gunsmiths found it difficult, if not impossible, to turn out components with the precise dimensions required by his breech-loader.

At this point, Hall came to a startling realization. To build his rifle he needed machines, not gunsmiths. He figured if he could invent the rifle, he could also invent machines to make it. And that's exactly what he did. To take the place of the armory's imperfect craftsmen, he painstakingly constructed a battery of water-powered machines which could crank out an endless number of metal parts each exactly like the last. This made the components interchangeable so that a part from one rifle functioned equally well on another. Building the rifle became a simple matter of assembling the various pieces, and unskilled laborers, even children, could be hired to do the work. Given the necessary spare parts, anyone could make repairs. In the field, a piece taken from a broken rifle could be used to repair another rifle.

Stubblefield disapproved of Hall's machines, not to mention his Yankee ways, and the superintendent's resentment soon flared into open hostility. So Hall moved his operation out of the armory proper and across town to Virginius Island, a mile-long finger of land beside the Shenandoah. There, in a small brick building, Hall perfected and installed his ugly but unerring machines.

Over a period of two decades, the Hall Rifle Works turned out approximately 25,000 breech-loaders. It could have produced many thousands more if Hall had enjoyed the full support of the armory superintendent and received the financing he needed from the War Department. The government always looked upon the project as an experiment.

Even so, Hall's little factory offered a product far more important than rifles—an idea. Eli Whitney visited Harpers Ferry and the rifle works on more than one occasion. Simeon North, James Carrington, Asa Waters, and other inventor-industrialists also made pilgrimages to Virginius Island, where they listened to Hall preach the gospel of the machine and watched his clanking, water-powered factory in operation. When they returned to their own factories, mostly in New England, they carried with them a new way of doing things. Using precision equipment to produce interchangeable parts, they founded what would become known as the "American System" of manufacturing. That system, which would later be epitomized by Henry Ford's Model-T assembly line, made possible the world we know— the modern world—and along with it—modern warfare.

The Fall of Stubblefield

Ironically, the U.S. armory at Harpers Ferry never fully implemented the Hall system. Workers at the armory thought of themselves as craftsmen. Most of them could pick their own hours, take time off whenever they wanted to, and work at whatever pace they chose. Not surprisingly, they were afraid that the introduction of mass production machinery would downgrade their craft and place them on a level with the unskilled immigrant workers employed at low wages in Northern mills. Probably they were right about this, but because of their resistance to change, production at the Harpers Ferry armory lagged further and further behind its sister facility at Springfield.

Although Stubblefield had pioneered division of labor in arms making, he shared his workers' strong attachment to their craft. Hall, on the other hand, thought mostly in terms of mechanical things, and had little sympathy for the superintendent's attitude. It is said the two men never passed a friendly word between them.

It particularly galled the superintendent that he had to share his budget with the rifle works, and he invariably blamed Hall for cost overruns at the armory. In 1826, he demanded a full-scale investigation of the "waste and extravagance of public money" at Hall's factory. The commission called together by the War Department to inspect Hall's operation issued a report filled with praise for Hall, his machines, and his rifle. At the same time, the stir caused by the investigation focused attention on Stubblefield's poor record as superintendent.

The Harpers Ferry armory spent far more money and made far fewer muskets than the Springfield armory. Officials at the War Department had come to accept this imbalance as inevitable, but they found it much harder to swallow the questionable business practices that came to light in the wake of the rifle factory investigation. To their dismay, authorities learned that Stubblefield devoted the majority of his time to his Berry Hill plantation. For months at a stretch, especially during the planting or harvest seasons, he made only token appearances at the armory, leaving day-to-day operations in the hands of his brother-in-law, Master Armorer Armistead Beckham. When hiring, the superintendent showed a distinct preference for men who had loaned him money or who owed him money and needed a job to pay it back. By far the most alarming revelation was Stubblefield's favoritism toward a close-knit group of property owners known locally as "the Junto."

The superintendent made a habit of passing out lucrative contracts to friends and relatives—most of them members of the Junto. An examination of armory books revealed purchases of rough-sawn walnut gun stocks from Junto loyalist John Strider at the outrageous price of twenty-five cents each. The same wood could have been had from a Cumberland supplier at nineteen cents. In fact, Strider bought those same nineteen-cent Cumberland gun stocks and sold them to the armory, collecting a handsome profit for serving as an unnecessary middleman. Pig iron purchased under another Junto "sweetheart contract" was equally overpriced and of inferior quality. Musket barrels forged with this metal had an unfortunate tendency to burst when fired, making them more of a threat to their owners than to the enemy.

At a stormy hearing in 1827, the superintendent pleaded his case. Yes, Stubblefield told the commissioners, he had indeed let contracts for wood, iron, and coal without advertising for bids—but that was the only way he could insure a steady supply of quality materials. Yes, he had indeed appointed his brother-in-law, Armistead Beckham, to the important post of master armorer and kept other relatives and friends on the payroll, as well—but all these men were first rate gunsmiths and exemplary public servants in the bargain. To the amazement of nearly all concerned, the panel of War Department commissioners accepted these lame excuses and acquitted Stubblefield of every accusation. The commission even allowed the superintendent to fire armory workers who had testified against him.

Even so, Stubblefield's troubles were far from over. He soon made the decisive blunder of supporting Pres. John Quincy Adams in his 1828 campaign against challenger Andrew Jackson. Having swamped Adams in the November elections, Jackson appointed yet another commission to investigate corruption at Harpers Ferry. This stony-faced panel turned a deaf ear to Stubblefield's impassioned denials, and he was soon forced to resign. Later, a charitable member of the commission sadly described the fallen superintendent as "an honest, good man who had been too easy, perhaps, in dealing with scoundrels."

In the Grip of the Four Families

Most of the "scoundrels" whose greed and corruption had led to Stubblefield's demise were members of Harper Ferry's infamous Junto. In fact, Stubblefield himself was a member. The Junto consisted of four interlocking families: the Wagers, who were allied by marriage to the Stubblefields, who were allied by marriage to the Beckhams, who were allied by marriage to the Stephensons, who were associated by business interests and politics with the Wagers.

At the head of this wealthy and powerful circle stood an aging dowager empress named Catherine Wager. To many she was a fine and gracious lady, but to War Department officials, she was a troublesome old tyrant with a venomous smile. Catherine Wager's husband, John, had inherited most of Harpers Ferry through his mother Sarah, a niece of Robert Harper, who had died childless in 1783. When the government bought up most of the town for the armory in 1796, the Wagers kept six prime acres for themselves. They also continued to operate Harper's old ferries across the Potomac and Shenandoah.

Since the Wagers controlled access to the town and held all the private land in the vicinity of the armory, they were able to maintain a tight monopoly on commerce at Harpers Ferry. No one could open or run a business unless he rented from the Wagers. If an armory worker wanted to buy a bag of flour or a slab of bacon, he had to pay fixed Wager prices, which of course, were always high. This amounted to a private tap on the U.S. treasury, since armory salaries had to keep pace with the cost of living.

According to Catherine Wager, the original government purchase had included an unwritten promise that only the Wagers and their lease holders would be allowed to supply

the needs of the armorers. She never lost a chance to remind officials at the War Department of this "gentleman's
agreement." During her lifetime, which extended into the
1820s, she made the arrangement stick. Men such as James
McHenry and John C. Calhoun could contemplate the
bloody clash of armies or naval warfare on a global scale,
but they could not bring themselves to stand up against the
old woman who ran Harpers Ferry.

In time, the Stubblefields, Beckhams, and Stephensons
each took a slice of the Wager pie. Perhaps the strongest ap-
petites among them belonged to the Beckhams, several of
whom had weaseled their way into bogus jobs at the armory.
Brothers Camp and Fontaine Beckham drew large federal
salaries from the armory paymaster but spent nearly all
their time running a lucrative oil mill on Virginius Island.
No one questioned the brothers about this arrangement because their uncle was Armistead Beckham, the master armorer and political strong man who ran the musket factory
as if it were a medieval fief—Beckham was the warlord and
the workers his serfs.

Under pressure from President Jackson's commission,
Armistead Beckham followed his old crony, Stubblefield,
out the armory door. War Department officials hoped this
would put an end to corruption at the armory and loosen
the Junto's grip on the town. They were disappointed. The
Junto survived because it was woven into the fabric of life at
Harpers Ferry. By accepting a job, a house, a loan, or a favor from a Junto member, a worker or merchant indebted
himself and cast a silent vote for the feudal state of affairs in
the town. The armory did not change much either. When
Armistead Beckham resigned, his nephew Fontaine slipped
quietly into his shoes as master armorer.

Murder in the Superintendent's Office

The War Department filled the empty superintendent's
chair with Col. Thomas Dunn, a respected militia officer
and manager of the iron works in nearby Antietam. Depart-

ment officials ordered the new superintendent to restore sound business practices to armory management. Dunn started by sacking several of the worthless workers who had swelled the armory payroll under the regime of Stubblefield and Beckham.

One of the dismissed armorers, a young man named Ebenezer Cox, refused to leave. Pushing his way into Dunn's office, Cox pleaded with the new superintendent to let him keep his job—he had debts, he had responsibilities, he had a family. Dunn remained firm and had him thrown off the armory grounds. That same afternoon, Cox returned carrying a loaded carbine—not of Harpers Ferry manufacture—and shot Dunn in the stomach. As Dunn lay dying, his dinner rice, eaten only a few minutes before, poured through a ghastly wound onto the office carpet.

On a frightfully cold day in February of 1830, Colonel Dunn was buried on a hill in Sharpsburg, Maryland. Some thirty-two years afterward, several thousand Americans would stain that hill with their blood during the Battle of Antietam. Coincidentally, Gen. Robert E. Lee is said to have stood near Dunn's grave while directing the movements of his troops.

Six months after the murder, Cox mounted a gallows in Charles Town. Before his executioners slipped the noose around his neck, the condemned man told them that Dunn's murder had been a conspiracy—but he would name no names. Afterwards, it was widely rumored that members of the Junto—jealous of their hold on the armory and on Harpers Ferry—had a hand in the murder. However, no one but Cox would ever be indicted for the crime.

The Junto survived the uproar over the murder of Colonel Dunn just as it had survived repeated attempts on the part of the U.S. government to dislodge it. But during the decade that followed, it withered and died as if of old age. A feudal system can exist only in isolation, and a major railroad and canal were about to open Harpers Ferry to the world.

The Baltimore and Ohio Railroad won its hammer-versus-shovel race with the Chesapeake and Ohio Canal. Here, well-dressed citizens pose on a wide-stacked B & O engine.

5

The C & O Versus the B & O

Hammer Against Shovel

Wearing a top hat and black dress coat, Pres. John Quincy Adams looked very much out of place standing in a weedy field just outside of Georgetown in the District of Columbia. An aristocratic man, unused to physical labor of any sort, he probably felt even less comfortable than he looked because someone had just put a shovel in his hands.

The date was July 4, 1828, and George Washington's dream of a navigable Potomac, a river highway to the interior of the country, was about to be reborn as the Chesapeake and Ohio Canal. President Adams himself had been asked to turn the first spade of earth.

The president was handy with words but not with shovels, and at any other time, he might have left this task to one of his cabinet members. It was an election year, however, and he was facing a hard campaign against his hated rival, Andrew Jackson, a westerner known for his physical vigor. So Adams was determined to show the assembled gallery of congressmen, diplomats, and gaily dressed Washington ladies, that he, too, was a man of action.

First he had a few words to say. Adams compared the canal project to "the Pyramids of Egypt, the Colossus of Rhodes, the Temple of Ephesus, the mausoleum of Artemisis, the wall of

China." He assured the crowd that these ancient wonders of the world would "sink into insignificance" before the canal once it was complete. Unable to resist getting in at least one dig against his campaign opponent, he ended his speech with a prayer for the nation. In earlier speeches Adams had warned that Jackson was a divisive influence, a man likely to split the country apart. Now he asked God to make the C & O "one of his chosen instruments for the preservation, prosperity, and perpetuity of the union."

Having placed the event in its proper perspective, Adams turned to the task at hand and put the full weight of the presidency behind his C & O shovel. Unfortunately, he struck a large tree root hidden just beneath the surface. If there were any Jackson supporters in the crowd, they probably laughed and jeered, but most of the spectators cheered the president as he doffed his hat and coat and rolled up his sleeves. Moving to a softer spot, he managed to scoop out a respectable shovelful of dirt and with a relief that was perhaps too obvious handed the shovel back to his hosts. Ultimately, Adams' heroic service as a ditch digger would not save him from being buried by Jackson in the November election.

The C & O was finally underway, and none too soon, for like Adams, the canal was locked in mortal combat with an energetic and implacable opponent. While Adams sweated over his shovel, some thirty miles to the north in Baltimore, a crowd larger than the one in Georgetown cheered a dignitary at least as well known and respected as the president. He was Charles Carroll, and in 1776 he had affixed his signature to a document requiring him to pledge his life, his fortune, and his sacred honor to a great cause—the building of a nation. Now, as the last surviving signer of the Declaration of Independence, Carroll lent his name to a construction project that was very different and yet somehow similar to the one he had helped begin exactly fifty-two years earlier. Wielding a sledgehammer rather than a shovel, the old man lustily drove the first spike into the Baltimore and Ohio Railroad.

The gauntlet was down. With the ceremonies over, the C & O and B & O raced westward to compete for the rich freight traffic—grain, coal, and lumber moving from the Ohio Valley through the Blue Ridge Mountains to the port cities on the eastern seaboard. They set their sights on Cumberland, Maryland, the coal mining center in the Alleghenies. Whichever reached Cumberland first would gobble up the lion's share of trade. To get there they had to pass through Harpers Ferry, some fifty-five miles west of Washington and about sixty miles southwest of Baltimore. But the road to Harpers Ferry proved to be a rocky one for both canal and railroad.

That root President Adams struck in Georgetown proved to have been an omen. The shovels of canal work gangs were repeatedly blunted by slate, gravel, and hardpan often lurking just below the surface of the soil. Lumber, cement, and other building materials were scarce and expensive. So were skilled workmen. To solve the labor problem, the canal imported indentured workers—stone masons from England, carpenters from Germany, and coal miners from Wales to dig tunnels. Digging the canal proved far more expensive than anyone had expected, and the C & O sank deeper and deeper into a swamp of unpaid bills and debts.

Better financed and with fewer technical hurdles to clear, the B & O made rapid progress at first, but success bred overconfidence. B & O lawyers stirred up a legal hornet's nest over a key right-of-way, and the infant railroad was the one that ended up getting stung.

A Tight Squeeze

Engineers for both the C & O canal and B & O railroad saw the narrow Potomac gorge above Point of Rocks, about twelve miles east of Harpers Ferry, as a formidable obstacle. At the same time, investors who owned the rival transportation systems looked upon the gorge as an opportunity to squeeze their opponents out of the race for Harpers Ferry and Cumberland. Here the limestone cliffs of the Appalachian foothills pressed in so close to the river that there was barely enough room for a rude footpath, let alone space for both a canal and a railroad. It appeared that one or the other would be able to go this far and no farther.

Recognizing the importance of this bottleneck, the B & O rushed its agents into the gorge where they bought up all the available land on the flatter, north bank of the river. Meanwhile, since they had inherited a legal right-of-way from Washington's failed Potomac Company, C & O officials remained confident. Shovels bit into the dark Maryland soil and hammers drove spikes into steel rails as canal and railroad drew ever closer to Point of Rocks. What would happen when they slammed into each other at the gorge?

The B & O was the first to flinch. They decided to draw their battle line not at the gorge but in court. The railroad had staked a strong legal claim on the gorge—it owned the land. After the B & O attorneys had presented its case, however, lawyers for the canal smiled and shook their heads. Surely the courts could see these newfangled railroads for what they really were—a pack of fanciful notions in the minds of some wildly imaginative mechanics. If a railroad attempted to haul a load of hay, would not sparks from the engine set it on fire? Rails made brittle by harsh winter cold would surely snap under the weight of a fully loaded train. A locomotive and eight carriages—enough to carry twenty-five tons of cargo—would cost upwards of $4,000, an unthinkable sum. Canals, on the other hand, were much more practical. A canal boat with a capacity of twenty-five tons could be purchased for a mere $100, and if a farmer could not afford to buy or rent a boat to take his grain to market, he could build one himself. No wonder that any number of beneficial—and highly profitable—canals already existed both in America and abroad, while the nation's first railroad was yet to be built. Canals were a fact. Railroads were an unrealistic metal dream. Or so argued the C & O.

The courts did not entirely fall for the C & O's folksy argument, but they did acknowledge the canal's long-established right to pass through the Potomac gorge. Although the railroad legal team fought on for nearly four years, the canal won. Just as the unlucky Robert Harper had to pay for his land twice, the railroad, which already owned all the land in the gorge, had to pay its competitor $266,000 for the right-of-way to build on it. Fortunately, engineers had worked out a way for the canal and the railroad to pass through the Potomac gorge side-by-side so that construction of both transportation systems could continue. But the B & O had to promise not to build beyond Harpers Ferry until the canal had reached Cumberland or until 1840, whichever came first. The terms of the legal settlement were harsh, but while the B & O had lost a major legal battle, the war for economic survival was just beginning.

The infusion of money from the railroad breathed new life into the debt-ridden canal project, and by 1833 C & O construction crews had extended their big ditch as far as Harpers Ferry. The railroad was just behind them. Early in 1834 a crowd of armory workers crossed the Potomac to cheer the first flag-draped B & O engine as it steamed into a temporary station built right alongside the canal.

Even with the help of railroad money, C & O construction crews found their work slow and tedious. The canal needed dozens of locks to raise it from near sea level at Georgetown to the 600-foot elevation of Cumberland. When 1840 arrived, the canal builders were still slogging through the Potomac valley, many miles from Cumberland. Released from its legal shackles, the B & O then launched its assault on the Alleghenies, and the first locomotive pulled into Cumberland on November 5, 1842. The C & O would not carry its first Cumberland coal until 1850, some eight years afterward. By that time the railroad, with its speed, power, and regularly scheduled service, had made its rival utterly obsolete.

The Chesapeake and Ohio Canal, that man-made, American-built wonder of the world, more impressive than "the pyramids of Egypt" sank ever so slowly into obscurity and extinction. Hit repeatedly by damaging floods, the canal

B & O switching engines at the Harpers Ferry station in 1910.

nonetheless survived well into the twentieth century. The last decaying canal boat made the 188-mile trip from Cumberland to Georgetown shortly before a great Potomac flood overwhelmed the canal in 1924.

Two Presidents Float to Harpers Ferry

In 1834, C & O directors had believed they would carry the future in their mule-drawn canal boats. During a late spring heat wave in May of that year, they invited practically the whole of Congress to inspect the wondrous new canal as part of a weekend junket to Harpers Ferry.

The journey began at five o'clock in the morning on what turned out to be one the hottest days of the year. A steamy haze was already rising off the Potomac when the congressional party—they brought along their wives as well as the entire Marine Band decked out in parade uniform—crowded onto a pair of canal boats at Georgetown. The sweltering heat combined with cramped quarters on the narrow boats to make this a sweaty trip indeed, and the slow pace didn't help. The boats could move no faster than their mule team plodding along on the towpath ahead, and they had to stop at each of the thirty-four locks between Georgetown and Harpers Ferry. To pass the time the passengers ate, argued, joked, and drank.

Among those who went along for the ride were a former president, John Quincy Adams, and a future president, Franklin Pierce of Ohio. If Adams had known Pierce's destiny, he might have passed along this piece of advice to the young Ohio congressman: When you become president, don't volunteer to break ground for any new canals. Adams's luck had been rotten ever since he'd embarrassed himself with that shovel at Georgetown. He'd run for re-election and been thumpingly defeated by Andrew Jackson, and now he was forced to suffer the boredom of a seemingly endless trek along the steamy Potomac. What was worse, he had to endure the company of a crowd of rowdy western congressmen. The refined Adams watched the westerners with distaste as the heavy imbibing of wine made "some of the company loquacious and some drowsy." Representative Hawes of Kentucky is said to have made himself particularly obnoxious with his coarse jokes and drunkenness.

The ladies who made the journey avoided the hard language and occasional rain showers by holing up in the cabin of one of the boats. There they entertained themselves singing Methodist hymns. The two boats, loaded with U.S. congressmen and their hoarse womenfolk, finally arrived in Harpers Ferry at nine o'clock in the evening. They'd covered the fifty-five miles from the capital in just under sixteen hours. Travelers would soon be able to make the same trip by train in a little more than two hours. No doubt, Adams resolved to travel by train ever after.

6

A Coming of Age

Fast Times at Harpers Ferry

After 1834, Harpers Ferry became a key destination for both a canal and a major railroad, and business boomed. Attracted by the wheel-turning power of the Shenandoah, an iron foundry, machine shop, cotton mill, flour mill, sawmill, and carriage factory joined the rifle works of crowded Virginius Island. The armory was expanded during the 1830s, and federal money flowed as fast as the rivers.

Finally free of the old Wager land monopoly and the dampening influence of the Junto, businessmen in town scrambled to siphon off as much of that money as possible. They hawked their wares in local newspapers such as the *Virginia Free Press.* In one advertisement George Glassgow offered hats for "$8, $7, $6, $5, $4, $3, & $2.50" and suggested that "Persons in want of Hats will do well to give him a call, as he is determined to sell low for cash."

A *Free Press* advertisement described tailor George Cutshaw this way: "he flatters himself that an earnest desire to please and an unremitting attention to business will enable him to give the utmost satisfaction to all who may patronize his shop." Cutshaw must have satisfied a lot of customers. Business became so brisk that he was soon advertising for "Three or four Journeyman-Tailors, of steady and industrious habits" to work with him.

The interior of a Harpers Ferry general store about 1900.

Of course, not every worker had the "industrious habits" Cutshaw was seeking. Likely as not, he and most Harpers Ferry employers read the following notice: "SIX CENTS REWARD—Ran away from the subscriber on the 7th instant, an apprentice to the Butchering business named Dorsey Horner, a stout male youth, aged about 18. All persons are hereby cautioned against harboring or employing him in any manner whatever. The above reward and no thanks will be given for his apprehension."

A man named Gibson owned a pair of canal boats christened the *Hugh Smith* and the *Andrew Jackson*. In 1839, Gibson placed an advertisement offering "a large quantity of Fish, Oysters, and Potatoes, which he will sell low for cash, if immediately called for. He will also make weekly trips to Washington, and furnish citizens of Harpers Ferry with all the delicacies of the season, fresh and in good order."

Bartholomew Sweetman saw fit to "inform the inhabitants of Harpers Ferry that he has commenced the Baking business in all its varieties. He intends keeping BREADS AND CAKES of every description on the most reasonable terms."

A barber by the name of Tiball told the men of Harpers Ferry that he had "a determination to accommodate, and a fine lot of sharp razors, he intends to shave very close for cash."

Arnold Stephens explained that he would sell his "Boots, Shoes, Hats, Caps, Trunks, & C . . . at prices as low as can be purchased in the Eastern cities. . . . I have the advantage of a reduction of rent in my new location, instead of an exorbitant advance in the rent of the room owned by Dr. N. Marmion, which I recently occupied."

William McCoy invited people "to call at my cheap store on the corner of High and Shenandoah Streets, Harpers Ferry." McCoy also placed this ad: "Official! War Declared at Last! I have just declared War to the knife against the high priced system. . . . My watchwords are Cheap, Cheaper, Cheapest!"

Without a doubt the champion price-cutters in Harpers Ferry were the Conrad Brothers who claimed they always bought their dry goods stock for cash and could undersell anybody. "This is no humbug," they said, "but the sold truth." It probably was the truth. The Conrads sold whiskey for thirty-five cents a gallon. Perhaps it is easy to guess what young Dorsey Horner did with the first thirty-five cents he earned as a butcher's apprentice.

In July, 1938, Isabella Fitzsimmons announced "to her friends and the public, that she has opened a HOUSE OF ENTERTAINMENT . . . where every attention will be afforded to persons favoring her with their custom." Apparently, not many in Harpers Ferry favored Isabella. Less than a year after her advertisement appeared in the *Press*, the Fitzsimmons "house of entertainment" was for sale. Its new owners operated it as a hotel and filled it with the engineers and laborers who were extending the B & O tracks westward to Cumberland.

The Passing of a Genius

The railroad and the flood of passengers and business it brought to Harpers Ferry were evidence that a fire had been lit under the boiler of the national economy. The entire country was in motion—everywhere people were busy building new things or moving to new places. At Harpers Ferry, John Hall had fed kindling into the fire by helping to start the first great American industrial expansion. Unfortunately for Hall, his achievements brought him few personal rewards. While industrialists in the North were growing rich by using his techniques for mass production, he remained poor. Hall tried and failed repeatedly to negotiate a more lucrative arrangement with the War Department, which controlled all his patents. A handful of associates, Eli Whitney among them, recognized his genius, but otherwise he was passed over and forgotten by the moneyed and the powerful. Whitney himself is often given credit for many of Hall's ideas and inventions.

After more than twenty years at Harpers Ferry, Hall lost his government contract for breech-loaders. Soon afterwards, he came down with tuberculosis, and in 1841, Hall moved to Missouri where he died, a broken and destitute man. Almost as an afterthought of history, his family prospered following his death. During the Civil War, Hall's son Willard became governor of Missouri and helped swing the sympathies of that state to the Union.

The Passing of an Era

Nearly ten years after Hall died of the tuberculosis he had apparently contracted on swampy Virginius Island, his old boss, John C. Calhoun, himself lay dying in the Senate chambers. As the Old South's most brilliant spokesman, the senator from South Carolina had always stood foursquare for the right of white-skinned men to own black men. The Constitution guaranteed that right, or so he had often argued. Now, during the debate over Henry Clay's 1850 compromise on the issue of slavery, Calhoun repeated that argument one last time, but not with his own voice. Too ill to stand or even to speak, he was forced to lie on a cot and listen as a friend read his speech for him.

Calhoun probably gave little thought to the words he was hearing. He had written those lines himself, and had spoken them so often in the past that he knew them by heart. Maybe his mind was filled with memories of his gracious home in South Carolina, which as a young man he had left in order to pursue his political ambitions. Or maybe Calhoun, an exceedingly proud man, was mentally cataloguing the high points of his long and distinguished career. From the War Department, he had risen to serve two terms as vice-president of the United States, one under John Quincy Adams and a second under Andrew Jackson (he was the only vice-president to serve in two separate administrations). As secretary of state during the John Tyler administration, he had arranged the annexation of Texas. Certainly among Calhoun's most powerful memories were his debates with

Covered railroad and wagon bridges across the Potomac as they appeared to an artist some years before the John Brown Raid in 1859.

Daniel Webster in the Senate, where so many times he had wielded his eloquence like a sword in defense of the South and its "peculiar institution," slavery. Maybe he was trying to think of some way to take one more verbal stab at Webster. It is even possible that Calhoun, now drawing his last painful breaths, was questioning his own convictions. He might have considered what Thomas Jefferson had said about slavery many years earlier: "I tremble for my country when I reflect that God is just." Whatever Calhoun's dying thoughts, it is doubtful that the name John Hall ever crossed his mind.

The senator from South Carolina probably never suspected that he himself had planted the seeds of the South's destruction. When he had hired Hall and sent the Yankee mechanic to Harpers Ferry to make his new breech-loading rifle, Calhoun had unknowingly set in motion the wheels and cogs of Northern industry. Though Calhoun's words were brave and his arguments perfectly crafted, they could not stop the growth of Northern industrial power, just as later, the brave men in gray and their brilliant generals would, at last, fail to stop the lumbering Northern war machine.

Riding the Rails

Increasingly, the hotels in Harpers Ferry relied on the B & O for their business. Each arriving train brought new life and new faces to the town. In 1853, a travel writer by the name of Ele Bowen checked into one of the Harpers Ferry hotels, probably the Wager House down near the B & O station. Bowen had ridden the train from Baltimore, and along the way, composed this lyric:

> Singing through the forests,
> Battling over ridges,
> Shooting under arches,
> Rumbling over bridges,
> Whizzing past mountains,
> Buzzing over the vale,
> Dear me! isn't it fine,
> Riding on the rail!

Bowen would later write a book called *Rambles in the Path of the Steam Horse* (published in 1855) in which he tells of his visit to Harpers Ferry. "There is grandeur in it," he said. "There is the serene majesty of nature. There is that which touches the soul. . . ."

Bowen saw the town much as a tourist might see it today. He scrambled up to Jefferson's Rock and viewed the "passage of the Pawtomac through the Blue Ridge." To Bowen, it seemed just as Jefferson had described it in his *Notes on Virginia*.

Crossing a toll bridge over the Shenandoah to get an up-close look at a picturesque rock formation on Loudoun Heights, Bowen was shocked by the sight of hundreds of decapitated crows. Hurrying back to town, he asked about the crows and was told they had been killed by bounty hunters. The Jefferson County commissioners, who were no friends of crows, paid a few cents bounty for each head.

Another rock that caught Bowen's attention was the famous stone face that time had etched into the cliffs on the Maryland side of the Potomac. There, in the stone, Bowen saw George Washington "wrapped in contemplation of the land." Some years later, the formation would remind other visitors of John Brown or, as was more often the case, of Abraham Lincoln.

At the time he visited Harpers Ferry, Bowen had probably never heard of the tall, skinny lawyer from the Kentucky backwoods nor of John Brown, who was already in Kansas stirring up a prairie war. But Bowen had one trait in common with Brown—a fascination with weapons. Bowen became so interested in the U.S. armory at Harpers Ferry that he pressed the superintendent for production figures. He was told that the armory had manufactured 13,400 muskets and 3,227 percussion rifles during 1852.

Awed by these impressive numbers, the travel writer waxed philosophical. In *Rambles* he had this to say about the musket: " . . . from the moment of its origin it is identified with the history of nations. . . . It has conquered peace and protected religion and virtue—but still it has killed. . . ." He had seen what Harpers Ferry muskets could do to crows. Soon, Bowen and the whole nation would see what they could do to men.

The muskets included in Bowen's figures were distributed to militiamen all across America. Within ten years of their manufacture, many of them would be brought back and put to tragically effective use at the very same little town where they had been manufactured. But Bowen could not have known that on the day he visited Harpers Ferry and toured its Federal facilities. Probably, he walked right by the tiny fire engine house at the armory gate, and it is unlikely that he paid it any special notice.

At the end of his visit, Bowen boarded the B & O and continued his journey westward. He probably gave no more than passing thought to the telegraph wires lining the tracks. The wires had only been there for a few years, but already they were drawing the world into a tighter circle. Men like Bowen had a poor understanding of what the telegraph was doing to America. Bowen made his living by looking out the window of a carriage and then describing what he had seen in a book to be published a year or so later. But if anything dramatic should happen at Harpers Ferry—such as a raid by abolitionists—the telegraph could flash the news of the event to most of the nation in minutes. For Bowen, all the drama at Harpers Ferry lay in its scenery.

A Drifter on the Canal

The same year Bowen visited Harpers Ferry, Franklin Pierce became the fourteenth American president. Like the nation's sixth president, John Quincy Adams, with whom he had floated to Harpers Ferry many years before, Pierce would serve only one term. In 1857, he was replaced by James Buchanan, who—probably through no fault of his own—brought with him a tide of economic distress. Business went sour all over the country.

The coming of hard times caused a young New England

mill hand to lose his job. Unable to find employment near his home in New Hampshire, he drifted south looking for work. More or less by accident, he ended up in Cumberland, Maryland, where he signed on as a crew member of a C & O canal boat. All the month of July 1859, he spent making the round trip from Cumberland to Alexandria, Virginia, and back again.

As an old man, toward the end of the nineteenth century, the aging mill laborer took pen in hand and wrote the story of his brief experience on the C & O canal. He didn't sign the manuscript, and today nobody remembers who he was. We'll call him the "Yankee."

According to the Yankee, he "drifted" on a boat named the *Caroline of Williamsport*. Probably the *Caroline* was much like the other canal boats, measuring ninety feet in length and fourteen feet, six inches in width. The Yankee said she was capable of carrying roughly 120 tons of coal.

He said the boat was powered by a team of mules that walked along a level towpath a few feet above the surface of the canal. The mules were "geared" to the boat by a long tow rope. The *Caroline* had a complement of four mules, but usually only two of them pulled at a time, while the other two enjoyed a leisurely ride in the boat. Often, when the boat stopped, the mules were "ungeared" and allowed to roll in the dust which, as the Yankee noted, "seemed to refresh them nearly as much as a half day's rest." The mules were minded by a pair of "tow boys," each about twelve years old.

The *Caroline* was skippered by its owner, Captain Coss, and piloted by his "bows man," a free black named Henry Butler but called "Pic" by his friends. Running a canal boat was a quiet, even relaxing, occupation, but there was always the danger that the boat might run aground on the bank of the canal or slam into the masonry wall of a lock. The Yankee was impressed by the skill Coss and Pic displayed in keeping the *Caroline* at the center of the canal and out of danger.

By his own admission, the Yankee had few skills of his

own to contribute, but he was a "better than average" cook and had a large stock of interesting stories to tell.

Good stories were a valuable commodity on board a canal boat, which crept along at two miles an hour for as long as the sun was up. There were a lot of empty hours to fill. The Yankee said the boat moved so slowly you could get off and "fish, hunt, sketch, or geologize" for an hour, and then easily catch up with your crew again by walking along the towpath to the next lock. Usually the boat would be there waiting to be lifted up to the next canal level.

The locks, usually spaced two or three miles apart, were the soul of the canal. Cumberland stood more than six hundred feet above the Potomac tidewater at Washington. To gain or lose the necessary altitude, a boat needed to pass through seventy-four separate locks, each of which raised or lowered the craft roughly eight feet.

The Yankee said he got off the boat at Harpers Ferry, where he "waded out to a small island, and made a rude sketch of the notch through the Blue Ridge Mountains." Recalling this in his book he wondered if "some of the villagers who saw me there afterwards associated me with him." By "him" the Yankee meant John Brown.

The scene at Harpers Ferry was peaceful on the day the Yankee made his sketch, but it would not be so a few weeks later. When the Yankee returned to his boat, probably at Lock 33 across the river from Harpers Ferry, he almost certainly came face to face with the gatekeeper, a man named John Cook.

Cook kept not only the lock but also a dark secret. Only a few miles away, a friend of his was hiding out in a farmhouse making plans for a day of violence. A little more than two months later, Cook would join his friend, John Brown, in a bloody attack on the United States Armory at Harpers Ferry.

John Brown's target, the Harpers Ferry Armory.
This old photograph was touched up with pen and ink.
(Photo courtesy of the National Archives)

A canal boat slipping out of lock 33 just across the Potomac
from Harpers Ferry. Raider John Cook lived in the house
on the right while working as a lockkeeper and spying on
the town.

7

Appointment with Destiny

"Good morning, Mr. Smith"

On the morning of July the Fourth, 1859, a Maryland man named John Unseld rode his old plowhorse along the wagon path that ran beside the Potomac and the C & O canal opposite Harpers Ferry. On that same date, some thirty-one years earlier, Pres. John Quincy Adams had turned a spade of earth and launched construction of the very canal that now stood between Unseld and the river. More than five decades previously, in 1776, fifty-six Americans had put their names on a document having to do with the inalienable rights of men.

Unseld probably gave little thought to the coincidences of the date. He had plenty of personal concerns to occupy his mind—the run-down condition of his mountainside farm, the possible failure of his scraggly crop of corn, the long list of things he needed to get in Harpers Ferry, and the small amount of money he had to buy them with. Unseld was not the kind of man who paid much attention to broad, national issues. But if he had been, his thoughts might have carried him beyond the confluence of the rivers, down toward Washington where the slavery question was stirring political passions and where—although he didn't know it yet—Unseld would eventually testify before a congressional committee.

Whatever their subject, the farmer's thoughts were interrupted that morning. Four strange men stood in the middle of the road staring at him. "Good morning," said Unseld. "How do you do?"

The four men in the road all did very well, thank you. One of them, a stooped and bearded fellow, stepped forward to introduce himself as a certain Isaac Smith from upper New York State. Two of the young men with him were his sons, Oliver and Watson. At their side was a young friend named Anderson.

"Well, gentlemen, I suppose you are out hunting for mineral?" inquired the congenial Unseld. "Gold and silver?"

"No, we are not," replied Smith. "We are looking for land." Smith asked if any land thereabouts could be had for as little as two dollars an acre.

Unseld was taken aback. Good Maryland farmland was worth far more than that. It sold for twenty dollars per acre, at least. "No, sir," he said emphatically. "If you expect to get land for that price, you'll have to go further west, to Kansas. . . ."

A few months later, during the days of confusion that followed John Brown's bloody raid on Harpers Ferry, Unseld would be very surprised to learn that his Mr. Smith had spent quite a lot of time in Kansas.

On Pottowatomie Creek

The name Isaac Smith was, of course, an alias, and such a plain one that a man with a suspicious mind might have seen through it. But Farmer Unseld was a straight-dealing fellow, and he had no reason to imagine that his new acquaintance was anyone other than who he said he was.

John Brown, alias Isaac Smith, alias Shubel Morgan, alias Nelson Hawkins, also known as Osawatomie Brown and Captain Brown, must have been startled when Unseld mentioned Kansas. Brown had chosen the alias Smith as a joke; it was one of the few names even more common than his own. But his need for an alias was no joke. Brown was wanted for murder in Kansas, and President Buchanan had

*A clean-shaven John Brown in 1856. Notice the penetrating
eyes.*

put a price on his head. So, for a moment, standing there right across the river from the armory at Harpers Ferry, Brown might have imagined his secret was out—but only for a moment. He recognized in Unseld a very ordinary and harmless man.

Brown himself was anything but ordinary—or harmless. He was, in fact, one of the great inventive geniuses of the modern age. Whereas John Hall, laboring tirelessly in his rifle factory at Harpers Ferry, had created a new and more efficient way to make weapons, John Brown had discovered a new and more efficient way to use them. Brown's invention was a new form of war that could be fought without formal declarations or even the approval of governments. Its soldiers were clandestine fanatics who wore no uniforms and directed their violence mostly at civilians. Their specialties were the ambush and the midnight raid, tactics similar to those used by common bandits. They could operate in small numbers and in secret because they rarely sought to conquer military objectives, aiming instead to influence public opinion and policy in the most dramatic way possible, through bloodshed. Mr. Unseld could hardly have suspected that the old man he met on the Potomac wagon road on America's Independence Day was in reality John Brown, the world's first true terrorist.

Like many of the terrorists who would come after him, Brown was an utter failure by the usual measures of life. Through the first five decades of his existence, Brown faced reversal and disappointment in everything he attempted except in the begetting of a large family—he fathered twenty children. He failed as a tanner and shepherd in Ohio, as a wool merchant and farmer in New York. His performance as a rancher in Osawatomie, Kansas, was even more dismal. But the truth was, Brown did not go west to raise cattle. Instead, his objective in Kansas was to start a war, and in this, he came very close to success.

John Brown shared another essential trait with many of today's terrorists—the thought of death did not vex him.

He was not afraid to die, and he was not afraid to kill. In Kansas, murder became one of the necessary tools of his new trade of creating war—a direct means to an end that justified everything. Brown's conscience—and he was a deeply religious man—did not trouble him since he saw himself as a soldier fighting in the army of a merciless Old Testament God. Increasingly, as his string of earthly failures grew longer, he had seen himself as a heavenly instrument. He thought he could hear the voice of his warrior God calling to him, urging him to action. And in Kansas, he found a cause that seemed worthy of his divine appointment: the obliteration of slavery—and of people who did not share his hatred of it.

Like many Northerners and a few Southerners as well, Brown saw slavery for what it clearly was, an inhuman and unacceptable form of violence committed against those who are enslaved. Opposition to slavery in America had been gathering strength for a long time. To George Washington, slavery was simply bad business—the master always had to pay for the slave's upkeep but did not always get a good crop in return. To Thomas Jefferson, it was self-evident that slavery contradicted the Declaration of Independence. Jefferson was troubled when he considered the future of American democracy. "Slavery," he said, was like "a bell tolling in the night."

If you take a map of the United States and pull it apart, the rip is very likely to pass through Kansas. By 1856 the ringing of Jefferson's bell could be heard quite clearly in the newly opened territories west of the Mississippi, especially in Kansas. The droves of land-hungry settlers who tramped onto the prairie from North and South brought with them sharp regional differences, not just over the question of slavery, but also over taxation, tariffs, and many other issues. They spoke with different accents, worshipped in different churches, and bickered loudly over whether the territory would enter the union as a Southern slave state, or a Northern free-labor state. Their hatreds seethed in the hot frontier sun, like parched grass waiting for a lick of flame to touch off a wildfire. John Brown saw himself as a man holding a match.

In May of 1856, a band of Southern ruffians provided Brown with an excellent pretext by ransacking the free-state town of Lawrence. Although destructive, the Southern attack was bloodless. But Brown's reprisal was not. Together with two of his sons and a small band of abolitionist followers, Brown descended on a small, rustic settlement on the banks of Kansas' muddy Pottowatomie Creek. Five men, none of whom had participated in the attack on Lawrence, were dragged from their cabins and butchered. Brown started the killing himself by putting a pistol to the head of a farmer named Doyle and pulling the trigger. Two of Doyle's sons and a pair of cowboys from a neighboring ranch were hacked to pieces with broadswords.

Shortly after the Pottowatomie massacre, a contingent of the First United States Cavalry captured Brown and his men. The cavalry unit was led by Col. Edwin Sumner who, for reasons that have never been made clear, released the Brown party without making any arrests. While in custody, Brown came face to face with Sumner's right-hand man, a remarkable young lieutenant from Virginia by the name of J.E.B. Stuart. Some years later, Brown and Stuart would meet again—at Harpers Ferry.

The Pottowatomie murders inflamed Kansas, causing Secretary of War Jefferson Davis to rush army reinforcements into the territory. These uniformed Federal troops eventually put a stop to the fighting but not before there had been many more attacks and killings on both sides. The intervention by the U.S. Army disappointed Brown, who had hoped to see open warfare in Kansas. He believed that war was the only way to destroy slavery.

Dodging cavalry patrols, Brown continued his assaults on pro-slavery factions. Brown needed money to keep fighting, so he did not consider a raid to be a success unless he managed to expropriate (or using Brown's own word for it, "liberate)" a fair-sized herd of cattle or horses from the enemy. Often the booty also included weapons. After one particularly successful raid, Brown picked up a captured rifle and stood for a long time staring at the stock. Inscribed there on a metal plate were the words: "Made in Harpers Ferry, Virginia, United States Arsenal."

In 1857 Brown took time off from the fighting in Kansas for a fund-raising trip to the northeast where he collected arms and money from wealthy and powerful Northerners such as George Luther Stearns, Amos Lawrence, Dr. S.G. Howe, Theodore Parker, and Eli Thayer. Brown told these people that he was a liberator, and they took him at his word. Farmer Unseld would not stand alone as one who had failed to see John Brown for what he was.

Over a hot meal at the home of Henry David Thoreau in Concord, Massachusetts, Brown explained his philosophy to Thoreau's close friend, Ralph Waldo Emerson. Brown said his twin guideposts were the Golden Rule and the Declaration of Independence. "Better that a whole generation of men, women, and children should pass away by a violent death than that a word of either should be violated in this country."

It is unfortunate that humane and lettered men such as Emerson and Thoreau should have listened without protest to such dark and bloody talk. That they did, was an indication of the level of anger by that time flooding the country. What John Brown said at Concord should have been taken as a warning.

Two years later, a much clearer warning was placed in the hands of John B. Floyd, who had succeeded Jefferson Davis as secretary of war. A letter posted anonymously from Cincinnati, Ohio, on August 20, 1859, contained all the vital particulars the government needed to locate John Brown and arrest him on a charge of treason:

"Sir,

"I have lately received information of a movement of so great importance that I feel it my duty to impart it to you without delay.

"I have discovered the existence of a secret association, having for its object the liberation of the slaves of the South by a general insurrection. The leader of the movement is 'Old John Brown' late of Kansas. He has been in Canada during the winter, drilling the negroes there, and they are only waiting his word to start for the South to assist the slaves. They have one of their leading men (a white man) in an armory in Maryland—where it is situated I have not been able to learn. As soon as everything is ready, those of their number who are in the Northern States and Canada are to come in small companies to their rendezvous, which is in the mountains in Virginia. They will pass down through Pennsylvania and Maryland, and enter Virginia at Harpers Ferry. Brown left the North about three or four weeks ago, and will arm the negroes and strike the blow in a few weeks; so that whatever is done must be done at once. They have a large quantity of arms at their rendezvous, and are probably distributing them already.

"As I am not fully in their confidence, this is all the information I can give you. I dare not sign my name to this, but trust you will not disregard the warnings on that account."

In one of history's most profound derelictions of duty, Floyd shoved the letter onto a shelf and forgot about it. Later, when hauled before a congressional committee to account for his failure to act, Floyd said he had thought the letter was only an elaborate fiction. It mentioned an armory in Maryland, and he knew of no such armory. If Floyd had given the matter even a moment's consideration, it might have occurred to him that there was a very important and poorly protected armory right across the Potomac from Maryland—at Harpers Ferry.

Rewriting the Constitution

It was in Virginia, not Maryland, that John Brown intended to strike his decisive blow against slavery. With a small band of well-armed men, he planned to capture the lightly guarded U.S. armory at Harpers Ferry and hold it until news of the raid reached the ears of Negro field hands in the surrounding Virginia countryside. The slaves would then revolt and join him—of this he was certain.

More than 20,000 muskets and rifles were stored at the U.S. arsenal, a warehouse across Shenandoah Street from the armory. Brown believed that once these weapons were put into the hands of abolitionists and black men, slavery was doomed. He envisioned himself marching southward at the head of an army composed of runaway slaves and militant Northerners.

As part of his grand scheme, he would carve out a separate abolitionist territory in the southern Appalachians and use it as a base for further attacks on the institution of slavery. He had already drawn up a constitution to help him govern this new, anti-slavery nation. The government was to consist of a president, vice-president, congress, and supreme court. There would also be a commander-in-chief who had absolute veto power over decisions made by the congress or court, so that, in effect, the government was to be a military dictatorship. Of course, there was never any question that John Brown himself would assume the office of commander-in-chief.

A Right Smart Lot of Shirts

Good Farmer Unseld, who was not aware he was dealing with a commander-in-chief nor, for that matter, with a terrorist, was more than happy to help John Brown, alias Isaac Smith, find a home where he could set up housekeeping. Unable to locate any land he could purchase for as little as "a dollar or two the acre," Brown settled on a modest rental property known as the Kennedy farm. It had a small two-story house set back a respectable distance from a road used occasionally by travelers headed for Harpers Ferry, about five miles away.

Brown had his daughter Anne and daughter-in-law

*The Kennedy farmhouse about five miles northeast of Harpers Ferry.
John Brown's secret army billeted here during the months prior to the raid.*
(Photo courtesy of Bruce Roberts)

Martha join him in Maryland. The women lent an innocent, domestic appearance to the Kennedy farm, and they did the cooking, housekeeping, and washing for the band of terrorists gathering at the place. The sight of strange men prowling around the house would certainly have aroused suspicions among neighboring farmers, so the raiders were forced to suffer through the long summer days in the stifling heat of the nearly airless farmhouse attic. But Mrs. Huffmaster, a barefoot mountain woman who lived nearby, couldn't help noticing the large amount of washing that the Brown women did each day. She said to Anne Brown: "Your men folks has a right smart lot of shirts."

The men who crouched in the attic out of sight of the prying Mrs. Huffmaster were as colorful and varied as the shirts that weighed down the farmhouse clotheslines. Some were idealists while others were adventure-seeking freebooters. Some were educated men while others were illiterate. Some were sons of prominent families and had known privilege. Others had learned what it was like to work sixteen-hour days in Northern mills under conditions even more harsh than those endured by most Southern slaves. Some had wives and children waiting for them in the North while others knew only John Brown and their fellow conspirators as family.

Several of the raiders were, in fact, members of John Brown's family. He had with him his sons Owen, 34, Watson, 24, and Oliver, 20. Two other raiders, Dauphin and William Thompson, ages 20 and 26 respectively, were connected to the Brown family by their brother Henry's marriage to one of John Brown's many daughters. Although Henry Thompson had fought with the abolitionists in Kansas, his wife Ruth steadfastly refused to let him join her father and his brothers at Harpers Ferry. Henry's place, she said, was with her and their two young children.

Perhaps the brightest man with Brown in Maryland was John Henry Kagi, 24, from Ohio. Kagi had high, arched eyebrows and hazel eyes that revealed little of the feverish activity

Owen Brown, escaped.

Francis Merriam, escaped.

Watson Brown, shot and killed near the engine house.

John H. Kagi, shot and killed on Virginius Island.

Charles Tidd, escaped.

Barclay Coppoc, escaped.

William Thompson, gunned down by an angry mob.

John Cook, hung for treason.

Albert Hazlett, hung for treason.

Aaron Stevens, hung for treason.

Oliver Brown, shot and killed at the engine house.

Jeremiah Anderson, bayoneted by Marines during the storming of the engine house.

Edwin Coppoc, hung for treason.

William Leeman, shot and killed.

Stewart Taylor, shot and killed at the engine house.

Dauphin Thompson, bayoneted by Marines during the storming of the engine house.

that went on behind them. Gifted with a very facile mind, he had taught himself both Latin and French and studied law and history, mostly on his own. Kagi's strong sense of logic caused him to divide the world into two separate camps, one that made sense to him and another that did not. Because he could find no sense whatever in the South's "peculiar institution" of slavery, he became a devout abolitionist. Kagi taught school for a while in Virginia, but lost the job when he started one too many arguments on the subject of slavery. Soon, Kagi turned from teaching to journalism and hurried west to report for several eastern newspapers on the turmoil in Kansas. There he met John Brown.

Only one of the raiders had any significant military experience, and that was Aaron Stevens of Connecticut. Stevens, 28, had fought in the U.S. Army in Mexico and against the Apaches on the high plains before joining the free-state cause in Kansas. He served as drillmaster and instructed Brown's men in combat tactics. Probably the most idealistic of the raiders were the Coppoc brothers from Springdale, Iowa. Edwin Coppoc, 24, and his brother Barclay, 20, were clean-cut and clear-eyed Quakers. Like other members of their sect, they had an aversion to bloodshed, but apparently they hated slavery more than violence.

Francis Jackson Merriam, 22, was born into a wealthy Boston family. His uncle, Francis Jackson, was widely known as a fanatical abolitionist. Merriam was an exceptionally ugly man with a glass eye and a face marred by a birthmark.

William Leeman, of Maine, was, at 20, the youngest of the raiders. Leeman had little education, had worked as child in a New England shoe factory, and, perhaps to escape the drudgery of the sweatshop, had gone to fight with Brown in Kansas as a teenager in 1856.

Charles Plummer Tidd, 27, had a background very similar to that of fellow raider Leeman. Known to be good with mechanical things, Tidd could boast little education. Like Leeman, he was a native of Maine and had joined Brown in Kansas in 1856.

Albert Hazlett, age 21, was from Pennsylvania. Tall, red-haired, and muscular, he enjoyed brawls. Some who met him described Hazlett as an "ugly customer."

Jeremiah Anderson, age 25, was raised in Indiana, but his family was Southern and, ironically, had once held slaves. A soldier of fortune and thrill-seeker, Anderson joined Brown in Kansas and afterwards followed him to Harpers Ferry.

The raiding party had only one foreign member, Canadian Stewart Taylor, age 23. Little is known of Taylor's background.

As might be expected, several of the raiders were black men or men of mixed blood. Raider Lewis Leary, a saddler and harness maker from Oberlin, Ohio, was part Negro and part Irish and also had some Indian blood. He was twenty-five at the time of the raid and had a wife and infant daughter back at Oberlin. Leary brought his nephew John Anthony Copeland with him to Maryland. Born a free mulatto in North Carolina, Copeland was the same age as his uncle. He had attended Oberlin College and was an exceedingly proud man who carried himself with considerable poise and dignity.

Raider Osborne Anderson, 29, was a mulatto from Pennsylvania. A printer by trade, he had been born free. Although he had not been personally touched by slavery, he held militant views on the subject.

Only two of Brown's men had actually known slavery. One of these was Shields Green, 23, an escaped slave from South Carolina. Brown met and recruited Green in Rochester, New York, at the home of Frederick Douglass, the famous black author and orator. Douglass had considerable affection for Green, whom he employed as a servant and valet, and tried to convince him to stay in New York. He warned the young man that Brown's plans were dangerous, but Green was impetuous. Speaking in the dialect common among Southern slaves, Green told Douglass that he had decided to change masters. "I b'leve I go wid de ole man," he said.

The last to join the ranks of the invasion force gathering at the Kennedy farm was Dangerfield Newby, a former slave who had been freed by his master. Well over six feet in height, Newby was both the tallest and the oldest of the Brown's raiders. The forty-four-year-old Newby was probably less given to flights of youthful idealism than were his younger comrades. Nonetheless, Newby had far more reason to fight than any of the other raiders. His wife remained in slavery along with his seven children. She had recently sent Newby a desperate letter urging him to come free her "as soon as possible, for if you do not get me, somebody else will. Oh Dangerfield, come this fall, without fail, money or no money. I want to see you so much, that is the one bright hope I have before me."

"Men, get on your arms. . . ."

Raider John Cook spent no time cooped up in the farmhouse attic since he alone among the raiders was not afraid to show his face around Harpers Ferry. For nearly two years he had been employed as keeper at C & O lock No. 33 from which he could easily spy on the armory just on the other side of the Potomac. Cook had won the confidence and admiration of many local residents. In April of 1859 he had even married a Harpers Ferry woman named Mary Kennedy. A high-spirited man, Cook compensated for his five-foot-five-inch stature with his wit, eloquence of speech, and knowledge of literature. Born to a wealthy family in Connecticut, he had attended Yale and studied law in New York. For the twenty-seven-year-old Cook the raid was a question of both ideals and high adventure.

Cook lived comfortably in the lockkeeper's house, a two-story stone structure built beside the canal lock. He seemed not to notice when Isaac Smith arrived in July of 1859 and rented the Kennedy farm a few miles away. Cook kept his distance from the farmhouse and made few contacts with his fellow raiders while all through the months of July, August, and September John Brown gathered his flock and prepared for his final, decisive assault on slavery.

Then came the night of October 16, 1859.

Cook was at the farmhouse that night. So were all the others: Kagi, the abolitionist teacher and newspaperman; Stevens, the Indian fighter and drillmaster; the idealistic Coppoc brothers; Francis Merriam, the one-eyed Boston Brahmin; Leary, the harness maker; Copeland, the proud student; Anderson, the printer; Shields Green, the young servant of Frederick Douglass; Dangerfield Newby; Jeremiah Anderson; Leeman; Tidd; Hazlett; Taylor; the Thompson brothers; and the three Brown brothers. There were twenty-one raiders in all, not counting "de ole man," Captain Brown himself, who looked very much older than his fifty-nine years.

John Brown called his men around him, spread the King James Bible open on his knees, and by the firelight began to read. "Remember them that are in bonds, as bound with them," he said, and every one of his young men knew exactly what he meant.

"Except the Lord keep the city, the watchman waketh but in vain." And they all knew which city he meant.

"And almost all things are by the law purged with blood; and without shedding of blood is no remission." This last must have made the Quaker Coppocs more than slightly queasy, but neither they nor any of the others spoke out against the violence they knew was approaching. They all believed the time had come for the shedding of blood.

A chilly autumn rain had begun to fall as the raiders loaded a wagon with a few sleek Sharps rifles and hundreds of medieval-looking pikes made from long-bladed Bowie knives attached to six-foot poles. According to Brown's plan, the pikes would arm the runaway slaves who, it was thought, would be too ignorant to use firearms.

At about nine o'clock John Brown put down his Bible and jumped onto the buckboard of the wagon. "Men," he said, "get on your arms. We shall proceed to the Ferry."

8

John Brown's Raid

Rifles at Midnight

For more than an hour the wagon creaked steadily toward Harpers Ferry over the same road Farmer Unseld had taken on the day he met Isaac Smith and his young companions. What might Unseld have thought had he encountered his Mr. Smith now in the rain and dark? Would he have said: "Well, gentlemen, I suppose you are out hunting for mineral—gold and silver?" Probably not.

John Brown drove the wagon while eighteen members of his provisional army marched alongside, their rifles hidden under their coats and gray shawls. They met no one on the road, and there was not much talk. At 10:30 P.M. the invasion force reached the covered bridge over the Potomac.

Cook and Tidd cut the telegraph wires while Kagi and Stevens slipped onto the bridge and captured its night watchman, William Williams. At first the astounded Williams thought the whole thing was a joke, but the barrels of eighteen Sharps rifles convinced him otherwise.

Brown posted his son Watson and Stewart Taylor as sentries at the bridge entrance. He had left Owen Brown, Barclay Coppoc, and Francis Merriam behind to guard his Kennedy farm headquarters where most of his supplies and Sharps rifles were stored. The rest of Brown's army,

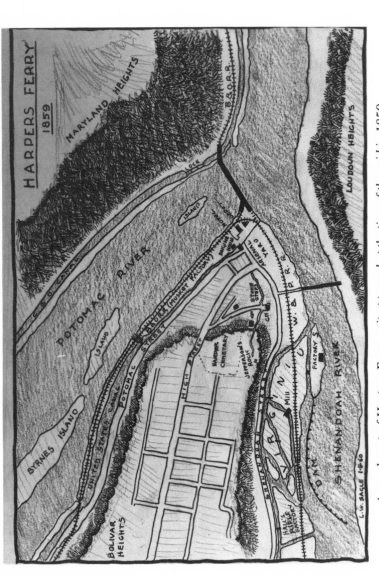

A rough map of Harpers Ferry as it appeared at the time of the raid in 1859. John Brown and his men may have sketched and studied a similar map before their attack. (Photo courtesy of B & O Railroad)

sixteen soldiers in all, followed him across the bridge and into the drowsy town.

At first everything went like clockwork. The armory watchman, Dan Whelan, was surprised and overwhelmed almost as easily as Williams had been. "Make no noise," one of the raiders warned Whelan, "or we will put you to eternity." Across Shenandoah Street from the armory, the raiders broke down the door of the U.S. arsenal, a warehouse for the weapons produced at the Harpers Ferry armory. Osborne Anderson and Albert Hazlett were assigned to guard it. Oliver Brown and William Thompson positioned themselves to block off the Shenandoah bridge. Kagi, Copeland, and Leary took possession of the Hall Rifle Works on Virginius Island. The remaining raiders fanned out through the armory in search of chinks and windows where they could make effective use of their Sharps rifles when the shooting started.

By midnight, the town bristled with rifle barrels, but strangely, few in Harpers Ferry were yet aware that anything was wrong. The first sign that things were not as they should be came when night watchman Patrick Higgins tried to relieve Williams on the Potomac bridge and, for his effort, had his scalp creased by a bullet.

Then at 1:25 A.M. an eastbound B & O train from Cincinnati and Wheeling chugged to a stop in front of the Wager House hotel and saloon which also served as the town's railroad station. Higgins, who had been hiding out in the saloon and bolstering his courage with liquor, shouted a warning, and the engineer quickly threw his steam horse into reverse and backed out of town the way he had come.

Baggagemaster Hayward Shephard did not hear Higgins's warning, and stepped onto the station platform in time to see the train steaming backwards out of Harpers Ferry. The raiders had not expected to encounter a man like Shephard in Virginia. Shephard was black, but he was not a slave. He was a free man with money in the bank. He had a good job working for his friend, Fontaine Beckham, who was the B & O ticket agent in Harpers Ferry and also served the town as its mayor. Beckham left his baggagemaster in charge of the station most of the time. Shephard had seen countless thousands of trains come and go, and could not imagine why this one was backing away. It occurred to him that there might be some trouble on the bridge, so he walked down toward the Potomac to investigate. A voice in the darkness ahead commanded him to "Halt!" Perhaps not comprehending, Shephard turned and ran. He had almost reached the safety of the station when a shot rang out and a bullet tore a gaping hole in his back.

Higgins ran out of the saloon and dragged the mortally wounded baggagemaster into the station office. Then, in a panic, he ran off to fetch Dr. John Starry from his small apartment on Shenandoah Street. Having been awakened by the shooting, Starry had already guessed there was trouble afoot. If he had any doubts about its seriousness, they were swept away by the sight of Hayward Shephard's ghastly wound.

Starry did what little he could for Shephard and then set about the business of raising the alarm through the town. First he turned three young men out of their beds, sent one scampering up the B & O tracks to stop eastbound trains and rushed the others off to alert the militia units in Charles Town and Shepherdstown. Then he hurried a friend up the hill to the Lutheran church to ring its bell. As people poured out of their homes in response to the bell, Starry tried to organize a resistance force to drive the unknown invaders out of the town. But to his dismay he discovered that in Harpers Ferry, where a large portion of the nation's firearms were produced, the citizens owned only a few rusty muskets and squirrel guns. In desperation Starry rode off to Charles Town to hurry along the militia.

The Sword of Washington and Frederick

The raiders could hear the bell and knew that the battle for possession of Harpers Ferry was about to begin. To give them an edge in the approaching confrontation, the raiders cornered unwary townsfolk on the street and hustled them into the armory yard as hostages. But otherwise, they simply stood by their posts and waited. They were confident, each of them believing that very soon the ranks of their tiny army would be filled out and overflowing with runaway slaves—that is what John Brown had told them. But except for the black men among the raiders themselves, the only Negro any of them had seen so far was the unfortunate Hayward Shephard. He could not join them now even if he had wanted to.

To get the expected flood of runaways moving, Brown ordered Cook to take a small party of raiders into the surrounding countryside to round up slaves. But the expedition yielded very little in the way of black recruits, only a handful of confused and frightened house servants. Apparently, few of the slaves understood what was going on at Harpers Ferry, and those who did wanted nothing to do with it.

Cook's men pushed their way into the home of a farmer named Byrne and at gunpoint demanded that he surrender his slaves. "If you want them, you will have to do the same thing we would have to do—look for them," Byrne said with sarcasm. Byrne explained that his two male servants had left the previous Saturday, probably to enjoy a night in town, and he had not seen them since. While Byrne may have seen humor in this, the raiders did not. They took him hostage.

Cook and his party managed to capture several other valuable hostages, the best known of them being Col. Lewis Washington, great-grandnephew of George Washington. The colonel had been in a deep sleep that morning, dreaming "of peace," when four men with rifles rudely awakened him. "Possibly," he said, "you will have the courtesy to tell me what this means."

Much to their discredit, the raiders stole Colonel Washington's silver and whatever else they could lay their hands on. The Colonel drew the line when they demanded his watch. "You shall not have it," he snapped.

Cook did not press the issue of the watch. Instead he robbed the colonel's weapons cabinet, taking a dueling pistol that had belonged to Lafayette as well as a sword that had been proudly worn by President Washington and, before him, by Frederick the Great of Germany.

John Brown took great delight in the Washington-Frederick sword when Cook brought it back to the armory along with his other booty and hostages. Brown tied the sword around his waist, as if to invoke the military genius of the famous warriors who had once carried it. Their skills would have been little use to him, however, since he had no real army to command, only an isolated band of amateur soldiers. By the time the first gray light of dawn broke over Loudoun Heights, Brown had still received no word of the expected slave uprising. Soon his raiders would be in desperate need of allies.

During the night, Brown had made a surprising command decision. He had allowed the long delayed B & O train to enter the town, creak across the Potomac bridge, and steam eastward. Soon, every telegraph office along the line to Baltimore was hammering out the news of insurrection at Harpers Ferry. At first, officials at the War Department in Washington were reluctant to believe the farfetched story of an attack on the U.S. armory, but before the morning was out, they were hurriedly mustering Marines. Troops in Virginia were on the move as well. Dr. Starry had ridden hell-for-leather to urge on the militia gathering at Charles Town, the county seat some eight miles from Harpers Ferry. By the time the doctor's lathered horse got him there, Capt. J.W. Rowan was already shouting orders to his Jefferson Guards drawn up on the courthouse lawn.

Meanwhile, the situation in Harpers Ferry was coming to a head. When chief machinist Daniel Young showed up for work that morning, he was denied entry by one of the raiders who told him the armory had been taken over in the name of God. Young thought for a moment, and then he said: "If you derive your authority from the Almighty, I must yield as I get my right to enter from an earthly power, the government of the United States. I warn you, however, that, before this day's sun shall have set, you and your companions will be corpses." Young turned on his heel, and with the providence that often protects the audacious, he walked away from the encounter. Others would not be so lucky. Soon after sunrise, a barrel-chested Irish grocer named Tom Boerly was cut down in the street by a bullet fired from the armory.

Recognizing that they were in a life-or-death struggle, the citizens of Harpers Ferry began at last to put their squirrel guns to use. Bullets ricocheted off the brick walls of the armory, and the raiders no longer ventured out from cover to take hostages. Gunfire pouring down from the hill overlooking the Shenandoah made things especially hot for Kagi's three-man contingent now cut off at the Hall Rifle Works.

As the morning wore on, Kagi became convinced that the slaves of Virginia would not answer the call to rebel. The raiders were on their own, and time was running out. Kagi was well aware that he, Brown, and the others would soon be facing, not just a disorganized local rabble, but disciplined militiamen and Federal troops. Dodging bullets, Lewis Leary ran from Virginius Island to the armory carrying a frantic message from Kagi to his commander, Captain Brown. "Get over the bridge and into the hills," urged Kagi. "Do not delay. Our purpose is accomplished."

Brown sent Leary back through the gauntlet of gunfire to Virginius Island. "Tell Kagi to stand firm," he said.

Dying by the Sword

Escape soon became impossible. Captain Rowan's Jefferson Guards crossed the Potomac a mile or so upstream from Harpers Ferry and then marched down along the same wagon road the raiders had used the previous evening. Shortly before noon they loosed a broadside of musket balls, let out a yell, and charged the Potomac bridge. The raiders standing guard on the bridge ran for their lives,

Oliver Brown and William Thompson to temporary sanctuary at the armory and Dangerfield Newby straight into a trap on High Street.

Caught out in the open, Newby had nowhere to turn, no chance to reach cover. Musket barrels sprouted from windows, doors, and alleys on all sides. But the former slave took a Virginia planter with him when he died. George Turner, a West Point graduate who owned a farm near Harpers Ferry, had just taken aim at Newby when the black man killed him with a single, well-aimed shot to the neck. In turn, Newby was almost decapitated by a six-inch spike blasted from the barrel of a crude musket. The spike, fired by Richard Washington, a kinsman of Col. Lewis Washington, instantly snuffed out the "bright hope" of one Virginia slave woman. In an ugly display of mob hysteria, enraged locals mutilated Newby's corpse.

Having carried the bridge, Rowan's militia took up positions at the Wager House and along Shenandoah Street, effectively isolating each of Brown's detachments. Other militia units closed in from the east across the Shenandoah bridge and from the west down the B & O tracks.

The U.S. arsenal fell quickly to the militia as its defenders, Hazlett and Osborne Anderson, slipped unnoticed out a back entrance. The pair hid all day in the thick bushes that grew behind the arsenal on the banks of the Shenandoah. Later, under cover of darkness, they stole a small rowboat and escaped to Maryland. Most of the other raiders would not be so lucky.

Flushed from his cover at the western end of the armory, young Billy Leeman splashed into the Potomac and tried to swim to safely. A bullet caught up with him about halfway across the river, and with great difficulty, the wounded Leeman pulled himself up on a rock. A member of the citizen army then waded out to the rock and finished Leeman with a pistol shot in the face.

The raiders on Virginius Island were pinned down by intense fire which poured in from several directions. Kagi,

Leary, and Copeland fought back stubbornly but knew they could not hold out for long. The decisive blow came when Dr. Starry, who had returned to Harpers Ferry with the militia, organized a company of locals and led a charge on the rifle works. The three defenders were driven into the Shenandoah where a hail of musket balls brought down Kagi and Leary. Copeland was captured alive and dragged to shore where Dr. Starry faced down an attempt to lynch him.

By the middle of the afternoon, what remained of Brown's invasion force was bottled up near the armory gate in a small building used for storing a wheeled pumper and other fire-fighting equipment. But despite the desperate nature of his situation, Brown still thought he would succeed or, at the very least, make a clean escape. He had ten hostages including Colonel Washington—about thirty others had been released unharmed when the militia attacked. He had support in Maryland—the three-man detachment he had left at the Kennedy farm and Cook who happened to be on the opposite side of the river when the Potomac bridge fell to the enemy. As far as Brown knew, these men were not under siege and might devise some sort of rescue. Most important, Brown still believed the slaves would rise up and join him, especially if he could hold out until dark. So the captain from Kansas turned to stalling tactics while refusing repeated demands for surrender.

In an effort to negotiate a cease-fire that would leave him in control of the armory, Brown sent Thompson and a hostage out of the engine house under a flag of truce. But the citizens, having seen their town subjected to terror by strangers with obscure motives, felt no obligation to respect white flags. Releasing the hostage, they made Thompson a prisoner and hustled him over to the Wager House.

Somewhat later, Brown made another, even more disastrous attempt to negotiate, this time by sending his son Watson and raider Aaron Stevens out for a parley. These two carried a white flag and took a hostage with them for protection, but the citizen soldiers now surrounding the armory opened fire anyway. The hostage escaped unharmed, but Stevens and Watson Brown fell, seriously wounded. Watson managed to crawl back inside the engine house. At considerable risk to himself, a hostage named Brua stepped out of the engine house, took the badly wounded Stevens in his arms, and carried him to the Wager House. Afterwards, Brua dutifully returned to the armory engine house to take his place among the other prisoners. Both the raiders and the citizen army that now besieged them might have taken this act of great bravery and humanity as a cue to stop the killing, but they did not.

Violence breeds violence. About the middle of the afternoon, Hayward Shephard succumbed to bleeding and to the great pain of his wound. Driven nearly out of his mind with grief by the loss of Shephard, his old friend, Mayor Fontaine Beckham developed a morbid curiosity about the raiders. Beckham peeped around the corner of a building one too many times, and Quaker Edwin Coppoc struck him in the heart with a musket ball, killing him instantly. Reacting to the mayor's death, an angry mob marched William Thompson out to the Potomac bridge and gunned him down with pistols. Thompson's body fell through the open bridgework and into the river.

After the deaths of Beckham and Thompson, a steady peppering of lead musket balls chipped away at the bricks of the engine house. Firing through ports punched in the walls, the raiders fought back as best they could, but the hopelessness of their situation must have been obvious to each of them. Darkness swept over the Virginia mountains, and still the slaves did not come. No one imagined now that they would come. All that remained for the raiders was to endure the cold, hunger, and fatigue—most had not eaten and none had slept for more than twenty-four hours—and then to die.

A spiritualist who had visions and made mysterious predictions, raider Stewart Taylor had bragged for weeks that he would die at Harpers Ferry. A bullet cut through the darkness and fulfilled his prophesy.

Another bullet tore through the wooden doors of the engine house and ripped open the side of John Brown's son, Oliver. Now two of John Brown's sons lay groaning and twisting on the dirt floor, both of them pleading to be put out of their misery. "If you must die, then die like a man," their father told them. "You will die in a glorious cause."

During the night, death had mercy on Oliver Brown, but Watson remained in agony. Gripping a pencil with a bloody, shaking hand, he wrote these words: "Fight on, fight ever you Hell hounds. . . . Lower your black flag. Shoot your dogs. Go in for Death."

The army led by commander-in-chief John Brown had dwindled. Of the sixteen men Brown brought with him when he crossed the Potomac, only four remained in a condition to fight. Nearing the point of total exhaustion, Dauphin Thompson, Edwin Coppoc, Shields Green, and Jeremiah Anderson watched through the portholes of the battered engine house as a second gray dawn set roosters crowing. They knew their raid on Harpers Ferry would be over soon. There were U.S. Marines outside.

Bobby Lee and His Marines

Less than twenty-four hours had passed since a Baltimore and Ohio conductor telegraphed this message to his superiors: EXPRESS TRAIN BOUND EAST UNDER MY CHARGE WAS STOPPED THIS MORNING AT HARPERS FERRY BY ARMED ABOLITIONISTS. THEY HAVE POSSESSION OF THE BRIDGE AND ARMS AND ARMORY OF THE U.S. By breakfast time on October 17, the first full day of the raid, this alarming news had reached the White House.

Well past the middle of his one term as president, James Buchanan had earned a reputation as an indecisive and ineffectual leader. On this occasion, however, he moved with uncharacteristic dispatch, sending immediately for his most trusted military commander.

Col. Robert E. Lee lived in a fine, columned house in Arlington, almost within sight of the White House, which stood about three miles away on the other side of the Potomac. A highly polished and respected officer who was educated at West Point and later had served as its commandant, Lee had impressive family connections—his wife Martha was a niece of George Washington. For those who knew him, who had witnessed his easy, aristocratic manner of command, it was not hard to believe that he would eventually move from his own mansion to the white one across the Potomac. But history took a different course.

Lee responded to Buchanan's summons in such a hurry that he didn't take time to change into his uniform. Standing in his civilian clothes he received his orders from Secretary of War Floyd: put down the rebellion at Harpers Ferry. From Buchanan's own hand, Lee also received a hastily written presidential proclamation ordering the insurgents to disperse.

Unlike Buchanan, Lee was by nature a man of action, not of words. He tucked the proclamation in his pocket and rushed off to do his duty. Outside the president's office he met an eager young cavalry lieutenant, J.E.B. Stuart, who offered his services. Lee accepted. Within the hour, Lee and Stuart were on their way to Baltimore where they boarded a special train, provided by the B & O company, and steamed westward. Lieut. Israel Green and ninety Marines had gone ahead of them on an earlier train and were waiting for them at Sandy Hook just east of Harpers Ferry.

By the time Lee and his Marines crossed the Potomac and took up positions around the armory, it was well after dark. So, for fear of injuring the hostages—including his distant relation, Col. Lewis Washington—Lee decided not to move against the engine house until light.

At dawn Lieut. J.E.B. Stuart, who would perform so many dashing and reckless exploits as Lee's cavalry commander in the approaching Civil War, marched directly up to the engine house and pounded on the door. John Brown answered the knock, and the sight of the old man's weather-beaten features brought a look of surprise to Stuart's face. "Why, aren't you old Osawatomie Brown of Kansas, whom I once had as my prisoner?" asked the lieutenant.

"Yes," replied Brown, "but you did not keep me."

Stuart handed Brown a note written by his chief. Standing within an easy pistol shot of the embattled engine house, Lee watched the old man read the words. "Colonel Lee, United States Army, commanding the troops sent by the President of the United States to suppress the insurrection at this place, demands the surrender of the persons in the Armory buildings."

Holding the note in his hands, Brown knew that escape was impossible. The slaves had not rebelled and would not be coming to help him. Neither would Cook nor his other men in Maryland, if any of them were still alive and free. But he also knew something else—that somewhere a length of rope was waiting for him.

"No," said Brown. "I prefer to die just here."

Lee had his reply. Stuart jumped away from the doors and signaled with his hat. Instantly, Lieutenant Green came running with twelve hand-picked Marines close at his heels. The Marines tried to batter down the doors with sledgehammers but only managed to splinter the stubborn timbers. So they brought a heavy ladder and, using it as a battering ram, forced an opening.

First through the breach was Lieutenant Green who had to climb over a fire engine the raiders had pushed against the doors as a barricade. Jumping off the engine, he brought the heavy handle of his sword down over Brown's head and hammered the old man senseless to the floor. Two of the Marines who followed Green through the opening were cut down by musket balls, but the others pressed on, pinning Jeremiah Anderson and Dauphin Thompson to the wall with bayonet thrusts through the chest and stomach. Edwin Coppoc, Shields Green, and the unconscious John Brown were taken prisoner and dragged out of the engine house.

U.S. Marines storming the engine house.

Under the command of Lt. Israel Green, U.S. Marines batter down the wooden doors of the engine house with a heavy ladder.

During the struggle, John Brown's prize, the sword of George Washington and Frederick the Great had fallen onto the dusty floor of the engine house. Freed along with the other hostages, Col. Lewis Washington reached down to recover his family heirloom and calmly walked out into the fresh air and the sunlight.

9

Aftermath . . . and Prelude

An Electrified Nation

The John Brown raid on Harpers Ferry was over. By any objective measure it had been an utter and complete failure. Brown had hoped to gather an army of abolitionists and freed slaves for a victorious march through the South. No slaves had joined him, at least none of their own free will, and a combination of local militia and Federal troops had quickly sealed off the town, contained the insurrection, and arrested the raiders.

In all, from the moment the raiders stepped onto the Potomac wagon bridge to the instant Lieut. Israel Green clubbed Brown senseless to the floor of the armory engine house with the hilt of his sword, the incident had lasted little more than thirty hours. During that brief period of less than two full days, the John Brown raid set off tremors all over America. It galvanized emotions in a way nothing had done before. Part of the reason for this was technological. Because of the telegraph wires that had only recently followed the railroads into every decent-sized town, news of a crisis such as the one at Harpers Ferry could now flash across the country at the speed of sound. In many places people learned of the event while it was still going on and *before* the outcome was known.

In the raid's very first act of destruction, Brown's men had cut the telegraph linking Harpers Ferry to Monocacy Junction and beyond to Washington and Baltimore. But by the next morning, telegraph keys at railroad stations in Monocacy, Charles Town, and many other locations were clicking steadily with news about the raid. As the day wore on and reports poured in, shocked citizens gathered outside railroad depots and newspaper offices in Atlanta, Richmond, Philadelphia, Boston—in fact, in cities and towns all over America. Dispatches were often read aloud to crowds shouting for the latest word on the crisis.

A throng outside the *New York Times* offices in Manhattan heard reports such as the following:

Dateline/Washington: ". . . negroes have taken possession of Harpers Ferry and now hold the Government Armory. . . . It is said that troops from Fort McHenry, Baltimore, will be dispatched forthwith to the scene of the disorder."

Dateline/Washington: "The latest account says the insurgents are Government employees, headed by one Anderson, lately arrived there. It is believed to be an Abolition movement to protect runaways. A large number of negroes stampeded last evening from several localities. It is supposed that they are making for Harpers Ferry."

Dateline/Relay House Baltimore and Ohio Railroad: "Gov. Floyd announced in the Cabinet meeting this morning that two months ago he received an anonymous letter stating that an Abolitionist movement was on foot, which would exhibit itself first at Harpers Ferry about the middle of October, but he treated it with levity and had not thought of it since. . . . A train has just arrived here with three companies but without ammunition."

Dateline/Baltimore and Ohio Railroad: "The insurgents have pillaged the pay office. Gov. Wise has ordered out the Jefferson Regiment. . . ."

Dateline/Baltimore and Ohio Railroad: ". . . one of the railroad hands and a negro was killed, while they were endeavoring to get the train through the town. . . . The insurrectionist number about two hundred and fifty whites, and are aided by a gang of negroes. At last accounts fighting was going on."

Dateline/Baltimore: "A late dispatch received at the Railroad Office says the affair has been greatly exaggerated. The reports had their foundation in a difficulty at the Armory, with which the negroes had nothing to do."

Dateline/Baltimore: "It is apprehended that the affair at Harpers Ferry is more serious than our citizens seem willing to believe. The wires from Harpers Ferry are cut and consequently we have no telegraphic communication beyond Monocacy Station. The Southern train, which was due here at an early hour this morning, has not yet arrived. It is rumored there is a stampede of negroes. . . . There are many other wild rumors. . . ."

Dateline/Baltimore: "Another account received by train says the bridge across the Potomac was filled with insurgents, all armed. Every light in the town was extinguished. . . . Men were seen in every quarter with muskets and bayonets, who arrested the citizens, and pressed them into the service, including many negroes. . . . Some were of the opinion that the object was entirely plunder, and to rob the government of the funds deposited on Saturday at the pay-house. . . . During the night the mob made a demand on the Wager Hotel for provisions, and a body of armed men enforced the claim. The citizens were in a terrible state of alarm, the insurgents having threatened to burn the town."

Dateline/Baltimore: ". . . the bridge-keeper at Harpers Ferry, perceiving that his lights had been extinguished, went to ascertain the cause, when he was pursued and fired on by a gang of blacks and whites. Subsequently the train came along, when a colored man, who acted as assistant to the baggage-master, was shot, receiving a mortal wound. . . . Feeling uncertain as to the state of affairs, the conductor waited until after daylight before he ventured to proceed, having delayed the train six hours."

Dateline/Monocacy Bridge: "The train arrived here at nine o'clock. Lucas Simpson, baggage-master of the mail train gives the following particulars: I walked up to the bridge and stopped, but was afterward permitted to go and see the captain of the insurrectionists . . . whose name is Bill Smith. I was kept prisoner for more than an hour and saw from five hundred to six hundred negroes, all having arms; there were two or three hundred white men with them. . . ."

Dateline/Monocacy: "The special train, with Col. LEE'S company passed this station at 11:30 P.M. It is supposed there is difficulty . . . as nothing has since been heard of the expedition."

Because of the speed with which this news was being gathered and dispatched, the reports were sketchy and, not surprisingly, laced with rumor. The delay in providing the complete story and in separating fact from rumor encouraged a free play of imagination among those who heard the reports. Because of the telegraph—invented only a few years earlier by an artist named Samuel Finley Breese Morse—the terrorists' purpose was being served in a comprehensive and efficient way never before possible. A seemingly minor, though violent incident was growing into an event of near cosmic importance. In fact, an astonishing transformation was already underway. The United States of America was becoming two separate nations, one Northern and one Southern, and it would take a bloody civil war to stitch them back together again.

As with many of the other terrorist leaders who would come after him, Brown's goal was an admirable one. He sought to destroy slavery, a morally reprehensible—and economically unsound—institution. But, like the terrorists of our own century, the means he selected for achieving his high-minded end was a dark and bloody one. Brown's planned march through the Southern slave states would have been accompanied by fire and violence on a scale unimaginable—unless one contemplates the death and destruction soon to be unleashed by the Civil War.

Although no one yet realized it, the first shot of that tragic war had already been fired. The war's first soldier, its first killer, was one of John Brown's raiders who stood on or near the Potomac bridge that linked Harpers Ferry to Maryland. In one of history's greatest ironies, the bullet he fired struck down the black baggagemaster, Hayward Shephard, a freed slave. After all, bullets are color blind, just as they are indifferent to status, age, sex, religion, infirmity, strength, cowardice, or bravery. Although few history books make note of the fact, it is perhaps worth remembering that Shephard was shot in the back.

Words More Deadly Than Bullets

A gentleman in all seasons, Colonel Lee refused to allow his wounded prisoners to be interrogated unless they gave their consent. John Brown, having regained consciousness, told his captors he was anxious to answer their questions. Brown had a deep saber cut in his neck and a puncture wound in his side, so he lay on a cot during his interview at the armory paymaster's office.

Among his questioners were Sen. James Mason and Gov. Henry Wise of Virginia and Congressman Clement Vallandigham of Ohio each of whom had arrived by train during the afternoon of October 17 following the storming of the engine house. Also on hand was Lieut. J.E.B. Stuart, who always seemed able to slip into any place where something important was happening.

Congressman Vallandigham asked Brown who had sent him to the Ferry. "No man sent me here," he replied. "It was my own prompting and that of my maker, or that of the devil—whichever you please to ascribe it to."

Senator Mason asked Brown why he had launched his raid on the armory. Captain Brown replied in a calm, matter-of-fact manner. "I think, my friend, you are guilty of a great wrong against God and humanity . . . and it would be perfectly right in any one to interfere with you so far as to free those you willfully and wickedly hold in bondage. . . . I

Virginia governor Henry Wise respected Brown for his nerve, but pushed to have the abolitionist leader tried and hung quickly.

hold that the golden rule—'Do unto others as you would that others should do unto you,'—applies to all who would help others to gain their liberty."

"But you don't believe in the Bible," blurted Lieutenant Stuart, who was not so courteous a man as his commander. Perhaps, he thought he could blunt Brown's verbal sword with sarcasm.

"Certainly, I do," replied Brown.

"The wages of sin is death," Stuart spit back at him.

"I would not have made such a remark to you, if you had been a prisoner and wounded, in my hands," said Brown. In an argument, the young hothead, Stuart, was no match for Osawatomie Brown who, despite his wounds, spoke with extraordinary skill and clarity.

Crowded into the room behind the politicians and soldiers was a phalanx of reporters from both North and South who would make sure that Brown's words reached the ears of citizens in every corner of the nation. The story of this debate between a wounded abolitionist and his slave-state enemies would soon flash out over the now repaired telegraph lines. Brown, who was always at heart a fire-and-brimstone preacher, knew he was delivering his sermon to an entire nation. So, he made the most of the opportunity.

"I claim to be here in carrying out a measure I believe to be perfectly justifiable," he said, "and not to act the part of an incendiary or ruffian; but on the contrary, to aid those suffering a great wrong. . . . you had better—all you people of the South—prepare yourselves for a settlement of this question. It must come up for settlement sooner than you are prepared for it. . . . You may dispose of me very easily. I am nearly disposed of now; but this question is still to be settled—this negro question, I mean. The end of that is not yet."

What the Nation Said About John Brown

Soon newspaper columnists, editorialists, and writers throughout the nation were reacting to Brown and his raid on Harpers Ferry:

"A bolder or a worse man . . . the world never knew. His single virtue, linked with a thousand crimes, was a bull-dog courage." (*Cleveland Democrat*)

"As I knew him, he was an even tempered man, neither morose, malicious, nor misanthropic, but kind, amiable, courteous, and gentle in his intercourse with men. His words were few, well chosen, and forcible. He was a good businessman, and a good neighbor. A good friend, a good citizen, a good husband and father. . . . He loved society, he loved little children, he liked music, and was fond of animals." (Frederick Douglass)

"Insanity is hereditary in that family. His mother's sister died with it, and a daughter of that sister has been two years in a lunatic asylum." (A.H. Lewis of Akron, Ohio)

"Editors [who said Brown was crazy] . . . seem to have known nothing about living or dying for a principle." (Henry David Thoreau)

"And they are themselves mistaken who take him to be a madman. He is a bundle of the best nerves I ever saw cut and thrust and bleeding in bonds." (Gov. Henry Wise of Virginia)

"That John Brown and his associates are fanatics is plain enough, but that they are insane . . . cannot be for a moment pretended. . . . The most that can be said for them is that they are men . . . who have allowed a single purpose to take possession of their minds." (*Providence Post*)

"The really wise men of the South will treat the whole affair as a most foolish, impracticable, and unfortunate scheme, planned and led by a brave, simple-hearted, unselfish, and modest monomaniac, whose heart has been lacerated by his own sufferings, and whose brain, touched by hereditary insanity, has at length become really affected and diseased." (*Boston Transcript*)

"The Harpers Ferry invasion has advanced the cause of Disunion more than any other event that has happened since the formation of the Government; it has rallied to that standard men who formerly looked upon it with horror; it has revived with tenfold strength the desires of a Southern Confederacy." (*Richmond Enquirer*)

"An undivided South says let him hang." (*Mobile Register*)

"The day of compromise has passed...." (*Charleston Mercury*)

Union on Trial

At the armory, Governor Wise had heard Brown's answers and decided on the spot that the man must be tried and hanged as soon as possible. Though wounded and unable to rise from his cot, Brown had fired off verbal salvos that could not fail to impress Wise, who loved fiery oratory and was himself something of a preacher. Such a man, the governor concluded, might prove far more dangerous with words than with bullets.

In a number of speeches delivered during the weeks following the raid, Wise described Brown as a leader with "courage, fortitude, and simple genius." The governor was not nearly so generous in his opinion of the residents of Harpers Ferry, who he felt had slept all too soundly while their town was taken over by a small raiding party of Northern abolitionists. In a thunderous oration outside the Wager House, he cursed the townsfolk as "a flock of bleating sheep." The honor and manliness of Virginia had been called into question. So, to show that the men of the state could stand tall, Wise was determined to see that Brown and his followers were quickly brought to justice and just as quickly hanged. The specter of the hangman's noose might then discourage any similar attempts to incite rebellion among the slaves.

Immediately following the storming of the engine house, authorities held only five of the raiders in custody, those being Shields Green, Edwin Coppoc, Aaron Stevens, John Copeland, and John Brown himself. Eleven raiders had been killed during the fight for the armory, while seven others had escaped. Charles Tidd, Francis Merriam, and John Brown's son Owen eventually reached safe haven in the North. But lawmen in Maryland and Pennsylvania soon caught up with John Cook and Albert Hazlett and hauled them back to Charles Town, Virginia, to stand trial.

Although the raiders had attacked a War Department installation, Governor Wise fought a successful battle to keep the trials out of federal court. It was a question of pride; he wanted the Virginia courts to handle the matter. So the eight captive raiders were hauled before a magistrate at the court house in Charles Town where they were charged with murder and treason against the Commonwealth of Virginia.

The first to stand trial was John Brown himself. The prosecution opened its case against him October 27, little more than ten days after the raiders had driven their wagon across the Potomac and into Harpers Ferry. Except for their unseemly haste, the proceedings were apparently fair. Brown was afforded all the protections available under Virginia law. Since he had no money to pay a lawyer—he complained that $256 in gold had been taken from him at the time of his arrest—the court appointed Lawson Botts and Thomas Green, a pair of local attorneys, to defend him. There was little they could do but argue mitigating factors: that, during the raid, Brown had not killed anyone himself; that he had not ordered the execution of any of his prisoners; that, in fact, he had taken considerable care to see that none of his captives was injured. When Botts and Green tried to argue that Brown was insane—their most likely and powerful line of defense—Brown fired them.

Hiram Griswold, a well-known Cleveland attorney hired by Brown's friends in the North, now took up the fight, but without insanity as a defense, he was helpless. The central fact of the case was inescapable: Brown had led an armed attack on a peaceable town, which had resulted in the deaths of more than a dozen men. In all, the trial took six days, but the jury needed only forty-five minutes to find John Brown guilty of the charges against him. Judge Richard Parker sentenced Brown to hang in exactly one month, on December 2.

Charles Town attorney Lawson Botts served as Brown's court-appointed counsel. When Botts proposed an insanity defense, Brown fired him.

During the weeks leading up to his execution, rumors circulated everywhere that armed bands of abolitionists were about to descend on Charles Town and rescue Brown. Hatched by Brown's most rabid Northern supporters, such plans did, in fact, exist. One scheme called for an attack on Charles Town by a hundred mounted raiders. Another aimed to kidnap Governor Wise and exchange him for Brown. The countryside around Charles Town swarmed with vigilant militia units, and these plans were abandoned as too dangerous and unlikely to succeed.

Even so, Governor Wise's aides reported to him almost daily on bizarre plots supposedly in the works. Absurd rumors circulated widely. Wise received the following letter from a self-styled "friend" who chose to remain anonymous:

> "I feel it my duty to inform you of a plot already matured too hideous and Satanic in its nature for a Christian people to tolerate. It is purposed that a Balloon shall ascend from the southern part of Ohio on the day of execution and taking the easterly current at high altitude and pass directly over the field of execution, and while in that position to cast over a large number of deadly shells, which on reaching the earth will explode with terrible destruction to all who may be in the way. It is also proposed to carry several barrels of NITRIC acid and pour the same on the heads of all who may be near the fatal spot which will surely blind and injure many persons. It will be the principal aims to throw a shell that may burst near you, Excellency. Take warning."

Another letter claimed that the governor and his family would be given a box of fancy soaps impregnated with a mysterious Indian poison. Wise made a note on the letter. "Such hoaxes put poison in people's minds," he wrote.

The minds of Americans were indeed being poisoned— by fear and hatred. In the Northern states that poisoning took the form of sympathy for Brown and his attack. Emerson called him "a romantic character absolutely without any vulgar trait." William Lloyd Garrison saw in him a likeness of Washington and Lafayette, and countless lesser orators sang his praises. Mixed in with the praise was no small amount of bile and venom aimed at the South. The rabid abolitionist Henry Ward Beecher (brother of Harriet Beecher Stowe, author of *Uncle Tom's Cabin*) described the South as "a great scowling slave state," peopled by "pygmies" and ready to unleash "armed hordes" to spread slavery. Whatever lay at the heart of Beecher's anti-slavery passions, it was apparently not any love for his fellow man—not even for John Brown himself. Beecher went so far as to suggest that "no man pray that Brown be spared," reasoning that Brown would serve the abolitionist cause far better as a hanged martyr than he had as a guerilla commander in Kansas or Virginia.

Meanwhile, the minds of Southerners were poisoned with paranoia. In the eyes of many in the slave states, John Brown and his raiders represented merely the tip of a vast iceberg of Northern conspiracy. Believing that their neighbors to the North had declared a secret war on them and their way of life, Southern politicians and newspaper editors began to beat the drums of disunion. In the Senate, Jefferson Davis spoke of the North as if it were a hostile, foreign nation. "Have not your murders already come within the limits of our borders?" he asked. A publication in Richmond demanded, in all seriousness, that New Englanders "be required to give security of their good behavior" before being allowed to take up residence in the Southern states. A newspaper in Athens, Georgia, warned "that the South can produce hemp enough to hang all the traitors the great 'Northern hive' can send among her people to stir up sedition and insurrection."

On the way to the gallows in Charles Town on December 2, 1859, John Brown handed his jailor a note. It read: "I, John Brown, am now quite certain that the crimes of this guilty land will never be purged away but with Blood. I had, as I now think, vainly flattered myself that without very much bloodshed it might be done."

John Brown rides on his own coffin on the way to the gallows.

Brown's dire predictions were right on target. What had been one nation was now two, and a conflict between them was inevitable. War had been a practical certainty ever since his wagon had rattled across the Potomac bridge, ever since a bullet had split the night and taken the life of a black baggagemaster. Brown had tried and failed to start a war in Kansas, but in Virginia he had succeeded. He had done what every terrorist seeks to do—he had violently reshaped the world in his own image.

Fontaine Beckham, the mayor of Harpers Ferry shot down by one of John Brown's raiders, left a will freeing his four slaves. These were the only slaves freed as a direct consequence of the raid. However, the rest of the South's slaves would be set free in the years to come as a result of the national bloodletting that was now unavoidable.

All the nation's people were about to be made slaves to war. Some of those who survived might look back on the War Between the States as an exciting and glorious time. But it was not so for the more than 600,000 men who died in the dust on countless battlefields from New Mexico to the Atlantic. It was not so for those who had their homes and crops burned or who saw their lives and families torn apart as the nation itself was ripped asunder. Perhaps John Brown glimpsed some of these dark consequences as he fell through the gallows trap to turn slowly in the mountain breezes of western Virginia—the other raiders tried after him soon followed him through that door.

Some hint of what the years ahead would bring could be found in the tremendous crowd that gathered to watch Brown hang. Among the militia units brought up to Charles Town to keep order during the hanging was one from the Virginia Military Institute. Its commander was Thomas Jackson, who in little more than two years would earn for himself the nickname "Stonewall." Another unit, this one called up from Richmond, had in its ranks a young actor named John Wilkes Booth. Legend has it that Booth entertained the restless crowd with juggling routines and quotes from Shakespeare.

10

War Clouds on the Horizon

Not One Vote for Lincoln

Eleven months after the John Brown raid, a hopelessly divided nation lurched toward the presidential elections of 1860. This was to be the nineteenth time Americans had picked a president. Always in the past, for all the heat and hard language of political campaigns, the selection process had helped unify the country. One reason democracies are strong is that the act of voting allows people harmlessly to vent frustration, fear, anger, and even rage while remaining faithful—and peaceable—citizens. Rather than cool people's emotions, the 1860 elections fanned the flames. Instead of choosing a president for all the people, it merely served to ratify the nation's division into Northern and Southern political spheres.

Among the strongest voices for unity had been the Democratic party, at that time the country's only truly national political organization. Predictably, the same forces tearing the nation North from South were also ripping asunder the party of Thomas Jefferson. The Democrats held their convention in Charleston, South Carolina, the city where John C. Calhoun lay buried. As if they were being urged onward by the ghost of Calhoun, Southerners led by Sen. Jefferson Davis of Mississippi tried to ram through a harsh, pro-slavery platform. Rallying behind presidential candidate Stephen A. Douglas, who knew he could never win the election while standing on such a platform, Northern delegations blocked the way.

"Gentlemen of the South, you mistake us," exclaimed an Ohio Douglas supporter. "You mistake us. We will not do it."

Unwilling to accept defeat of their platform, Southern delegates stormed out of the convention. Now there were two Democratic parties. The Southern faction nominated John C. Breckinridge as their presidential candidate. The Northern Democrats nominated Douglas. Yet another presidential hopeful, John Bell of Tennessee, headed a political concoction known as the Constitutional Union party, and ran on a platform of national conciliation. Meanwhile, the brash, young anti-slavery Republican party remained perfectly unified behind its presidential candidate, the tall and gangly westerner, Abraham Lincoln.

At first, residents of Harpers Ferry paid scant attention to all these political rumblings. The drama now playing on the national political stage had already been acted out—in all too violent a fashion—in their own streets. Several of their neighbors, who little more than a year earlier had laughed and drank and passed the time with them, now lay alongside old Robert Harper in the cemetery above Jefferson's Rock. The walls of the armory engine house and many other buildings were still pocked and scarred by bullets. The people of *this* little town would just as soon have forgotten about the slavery issue and the passions it had ignited. Nonetheless, when the day of the election came, they dutifully trudged to the polls and cast their ballots.

No one in Harpers Ferry voted for Mr. Lincoln in 1860. In fact, the Republican ticket received not a single vote in all of Jefferson County and only a bare handful throughout the entire state of Virginia—the Old Dominion threw its electoral support to Bell, the compromise candidate. Across the nation Lincoln polled 1,866,452 votes, less than forty percent of the total, but it was enough to win the White House. Douglas could muster only 1,375,157 votes, or about twenty-nine percent, while Breckinridge and Bell divided the remainder. Sweeping most of the Northern and Western states, Lincoln piled up a comfortable majority in the electoral college.

It is unlikely that Lincoln, as president of a united America, would have done much damage to either the South as a region or to slavery as an institution. In fact, Lincoln had made it clear that he sought only to stop the spread of slavery, not to abolish it in states where it already existed. Whatever Lincoln's intentions, the hostile majority in Congress and the Supreme Court, which was packed with judges sympathetic to the South, almost certainly would have tied his hands. But Southern statesmen heard the election results as the tolling of a bell—the time had come for the South to go it alone. Within a month after the election, the states of the South began one by one to vote themselves out of the Union. South Carolina was the first to go—on December 20, 1860. Virginia was among the last.

The secessionist movement alarmed many Southerners who considered themselves patriotic Unionists. Alexander Stephens of Georgia fought a lonely and unsuccessful battle to keep his state in the Union. Having lost the fight, Stephens shook his head and predicted gloomily that "men will be cutting one another's throats in a little while." Ironically, within a few weeks Stephens was elected to serve under President Jefferson Davis as vice-president of the Confederacy.

Armory in Flames

With the Southern states falling like dominoes into secession, Alfred Barbour, superintendent of the U.S. armory at Harpers Ferry, fired off a panicky letter to his superiors in Washington. Barbour had already witnessed one assault on the armory. Now he feared another. "I have reason to apprehend that some assault will be made," he said in a letter to Capt. William Mayberry at the Ordnance Bureau. "My reasons I do not feel at liberty to disclose. . . . But the Armory might be taken and destroyed."

Mayberry responded swiftly to Barbour's warning. Within a few days a small Federal infantry detachment arrived at Harpers Ferry and set up a barracks in one of the armory buildings. The attack Barbour had feared did not materialize, and for several weeks the troops had little or nothing to do. They had been ordered to make no overt show of force that might inflame local feelings. Emotions were running high, and the town was viewed by some as a powder keg waiting to explode.

The citizens of Harpers Ferry, like the population of Virginia as a whole, were about evenly divided on the question of secession. When it came time to elect a representative to attend the Richmond convention called to consider secession, Harpers Ferry residents sided with other Jefferson County voters in rejecting two candidates who had vowed to drag Virginia out of the Union. Instead the county's voters selected, of all people, Superintendent Barbour, who struck a more moderate pose. To avoid any appearance of conflict of interest, Barbour officially resigned his position at the armory. Then, just before departing for Richmond, he sought the opinion of a young friend and confidant named Joseph Barry. "What is your advice," asked Barbour, who was still not sure how he would vote at the convention.

No American village worthy of mention would be complete without a philosopher, a person who seems to have little else to do other than to dwell upon the human condition. In Harpers Ferry, Joseph Barry filled this office. As the town's self-appointed chronicler and historian, he never held a steady job for any length of time. But Harpers Ferry gave him plenty to *think* about. He had witnessed floods of biblical proportions, seen industrial geniuses come and go at the armory, and just missed having his scalp creased by one of John Brown's raiders. As Barry himself might have put it, he lived in "interesting times."

Never at a loss for an opinion, Barry was ready with

Like many Southerners, armory superintendent Alfred Barbour was at first lukewarm to secession. Later he rallied towns-people to seize the weapons factory for the Confederacy.

advice for his friend. Barry told Barbour he had "a fine chance to immortalize" himself by taking a Unionist stand. Assuming, perhaps, that most of the convention delegates would support secession, Barry reasoned that Barbour would rise above the crowd and attract national attention if he spoke in favor of Union. However, any visions of mercurial fame Barbour may have entertained quickly evaporated when he arrived in Richmond and discovered a strongly pro-Union convention. Maybe every town in the state had a Joseph Barry.

It seemed that Virginia might, after all, remain with the Union. Then the unimaginable happened. Shells began to fall on Fort Sumter, just outside Charleston, South Carolina. Delegates to the Richmond convention collectively sucked in their breath. On April 14, 1861, the fort surrendered to jubilant South Carolina militia. On the following day, President Lincoln called for 75,000 volunteers to quell what he was now calling an armed rebellion. On the day after that event, John Letcher, who had recently replaced Wise as governor of Virginia, sent a strongly worded note to Lincoln refusing to ante his state's quota of troops. War was clearly on the way. Convention delegates, including Barbour, were swept up in a tide of secession.

Barbour spent much of the evening of April 16 in a smoke-filled room at the Richmond Exchange Hotel where a clutch of Virginians plotted to seize the U.S. armory and arsenal at Harpers Ferry. Mastermind of the plan was ex-governor Wise who, ironically, had seen to it that John Brown hang for hatching a similar conspiracy. Everyone in the room was certain that, when the convention went into session again the next morning, delegates would vote to pull the Commonwealth of Virginia out of the Union. Wise knew the Commonwealth would need an army—and an armory—to secure its independence. So, he made sure that, by the time the historic—some would say tragic—vote was taken, militia companies were already moving by road and train toward Harpers Ferry. Wise told his friends that he

Virginia militiamen rendezvous at Halltown to march on Harpers Ferry. They hoped to reach the all-important armory and arsenal before Federal troops could destroy them.

expected "a fight or a foot-race between volunteers of Virginia and Federal troops. . . ."

One of the militia units on the march toward the meeting place of the Potomac and Shenandoah was the Jefferson Guards, which had sprung the trap on John Brown at Harpers Ferry. Among the officers marching with the Guards was Lawson Botts who had defended John Brown during his trial at Charles Town. A friend saw Botts in the street and begged him not to "draw your sword against your country."

His friend's emotional outburst had an impact on Botts, who replied: "Great God! I would willingly give my life to know at this moment what course I ought to pursue and where my duty lies."

Like much of the country at this sad juncture, Botts and his fellow Guards were caught in a whirlwind of doubt. For that reason, they did not move with the speed and determination that eighteen months earlier had allowed them to cut off John Brown's escape route across the Potomac. If the Guards had moved faster on this occasion, the fate of the armory and perhaps of the new-born Confederacy as well, might have been different.

Barbour reached Harpers Ferry well in advance of the militia. The town's secessionists treated him to a hero's welcome, but his encounter with Joseph Barry was somewhat less heroic. The sheepish Barbour had only three words for his young friend—"You were right." This remark left Barry with the lifelong impression that Barbour deeply regretted the turn events had taken.

Whatever his true feelings, Barbour continued to play his pro-secessionist role with apparent enthusiasm. Calling aside his former employees, the ex-superintendent urged them to support the Southern cause by guarding the armory shops and equipment and turning them over safely to Virginia authorities. However, the fate of the U.S. armory and arsenal was not to be determined by either its workers or their ex-boss. Instead, it rested squarely in the hands of

Lieut. Roger Jones, commander of the armory garrison that had been sent some weeks earlier at Barbour's request.

In the ten years since he had graduated near the bottom of his class at West Point, Jones had done little to impress his superiors. Until recently he had served with the United States Mounted Rifles, a regiment known widely as a dumping ground and dead-end assignment for unpromising young officers. However, when word of the vote for secession in Richmond reached Harpers Ferry, Jones acted with uncharacteristic military efficiency and resolve. With fist fights between pro-Union and pro-secession residents breaking out in the streets and confusion seizing the town, Lieutenant Jones moved swiftly, deploying his forty-five infantrymen to strategic positions within the federal complex. Knowing that he could not hold out for long against a sizable force, he had his men scatter firewood throughout the main armory and arsenal buildings and then lay trains of gunpowder over the floors. If Jones could not defend the Federal property in his charge, then he would destroy it.

Several of the town's more devout Unionists offered to help Jones and his men defend the armory. Among them was William Wilson who had tried to speak but was shouted down when Barbour addressed the armory workers. Jones sent Wilson to Bolivar Heights to watch for approaching Southern militia. Shortly before 10 P.M. on April 18, Wilson sent back a frantic message warning that as many as 3,000 troops (actually the number was closer to 1,500) were converging on Harpers Ferry from the south and west. An advance force of 300 infantrymen were within a mile—less than half-an-hour's march from the armory. Jones decided he could wait no longer. He gave the order to light the powder trains. Then, he and his men retreated into Maryland across the Potomac bridge. Virginia militiamen, who had reached Bolivar Heights and could see the flames of the burning buildings, knew by now that they had moved too slowly.

With fire-fighting equipment pulled from the same engine house where John Brown had made his last stand, scurrying citizens managed to douse the flames in the main musket factory buildings. However, shaken repeatedly by exploding kegs of gunpowder, the U.S. arsenal could not be saved. Stored in the arsenal were upwards of 15,000 new muskets and rifles, desperately needed by both sides—but especially the Confederacy—in a war that was growing hotter by the minute. The arsenal held enough weapons to arm nearly three divisions, almost half an army the size of those that would soon be facing one another at Bull Run. But none of its muskets would ever be loaded and fired at an enemy. The arsenal inferno burned with such heat that the barrels of some of the guns stored there melted and fused together into lumps.

Wilson and other Unionists who had assisted Lieutenant Jones in his hasty work of destruction now had to flee as angry citizens threatened to string them up. A noisy crowd demanded that a local posse be raised to set off in pursuit of Jones and his fellow arsonists. Perhaps the posse would even march down to Washington and "jerk old Abe Lincoln out of the White House." However, someone suggested that the Potomac bridge might be mined and for most that brought the adventures of the night to an end.

Fuss and Feathers

The flag of the United States was lowered from the armory pole and the flag of Virginia raised in its place. During the opening weeks of the war, Harpers Ferry became one of Virginia's largest military garrisons—almost 3,000 men, most of them reservists or militiamen with little training. They wore uniforms of every cut and color, and some wore no uniforms at all. A highly disproportionate number of them were officers, or claimed to be, and strutting around in their fine hats, they put on a daily show of what some locals described as "fuss and feathers."

By coincidence, the first commander of the Virginia garrison at the Ferry was militia general Kenton Harper of Staunton—no relation to Robert Harper. General Harper was a gracious man who considered it his duty to share a sociable glass of whiskey with any man who entered his tent—he had dozens of visitors every day. As a consequence the General was often too drunk to show his face in public. Harper led his men into battle just once when his soldiers fired on a B & O train believed to be carrying Federal troops. The train was stopped, but a thorough search turned up only one old soldier, an elderly general named William Harney who had been curled up asleep on a pile of mail bags.

Unlike many of his less sensible countrymen, Harney wanted no part of the brother-against-brother war that had just erupted. In fact, he was on his way to Washington to resign his commission, after which he intended to take ship to Europe. His uniform wrinkled and dusty, Harney was taken to headquarters where General Harper put a glass of whiskey in his hand and invited him to spend the night. The next morning when Harney got a look at Harper's motley brigades, he smiled and asked: "Where is your army encamped, General?"

Embarrassed by the unkempt and amateurish appearance of his troops, Harper could only spread his hands. "Excuse me from giving information," he said.

"Pardon me for asking an improper question," replied the old man with a twinkle in his eye. "I had forgotten I was a prisoner." On orders from Governor Letcher, Harney was released. The antique general was so old and so determined not to fight that it seemed unlikely he could do much good or harm on either side.

JACKSON'S BATTERY AT HARPER'S FERRY, ERECTED ON THE HEIGHT OF OVERLOOKING THE TOWN AND COMMANDING THE RAILROAD BRIDGE, CANAL, &c.—FROM A SKETCH MADE WITH A PASS SENT BY OUR SPECIAL ARTIST.—See Plate 12.

Stonewall Jackson's "apostolic cannon," dubbed "Matthew, Mark, Luke, and John," command the railroad bridge over the Potomac.

11

Between Two Armies

Jackson and Jeb

In Richmond, heads more sober than Harper's were coming to the conclusion that the South could not be defended with tipsy generals dressed in plumed hats. The Virginia military was placed in the capable hands of Robert E. Lee, who had put an end to the John Brown raid on Harpers Ferry and, without meaning to, had thus played such an important role in the breakup of the Union and the making of the Confederacy. Lee in turn named Tom Jackson to replace Harper as commander of the vital garrison at the fork of the Shenandoah and Potomac. Jackson put J.E.B. Stuart at the head of his cavalry.

A devout Christian and teetotaler, Jackson imposed tight discipline on his ill-trained regiments, banishing liquor from his camp and drilling his men upwards of seven hours a day. An artillery instructor at Virginia Military Institute, Jackson brought most of his students with him to the Ferry, and each day they wheeled four old cannon—legend has it the guns were nicknamed Matthew, Mark, Luke, and John—out of a church basement for gunnery drill.

Much of the armory's weapons-making machinery was still intact thanks to the bucket brigades of residents who had saved most of the musket factory buildings from the fires set by Lieutenant Jones's detachment. Jackson had the machinery dismantled and shipped southward to Fayetteville, North Carolina, where it continued to crank out parts for Confederate muskets throughout the war.

Jackson also devised a plan to provide the Confederacy with sorely needed railroad equipment. The B & O had continued to run coal trains through Harpers Ferry, just as if the country were not caught up in a great civil war. Jackson agreed to let the trains keep rolling, but complained to railroad officials that the rumbling engines disturbed his troops, especially at night. He suggested the B & O change its schedules so that all the trains pass through town convoy-style during a brief two-hour stretch from 11:00 A.M. to 1:00 P.M. each day. The railroad's management felt it had no choice but to comply.

Jackson waited until the new system was running smoothly, then he sprang his trap. The Confederates blocked off a twenty-mile stretch of track at noon one day and captured fifty-six locomotives as well as three hundred boxcars and gondolas. There were no tracks connecting that section of the B & O with any of the railroads controlled by the Southerners. So Jackson had fourteen of the engines loaded onto huge wagons and hauled southward through the Shenandoah Valley by thirty-two-horse teams. The other engines and rolling stock were burned. Soldiers piled thousands of cords of wood around the engines and set them ablaze. Hot air escaping through their whistles caused the engines to wail as if they were living victims in the last agonies of death. The eerie shrieks went on for hours until the fires had burned out. An old black man who had witnessed the spectacle gave thanks to God that the engines were finally "out of their misery."

During the early days of his stay at the Ferry, Jackson had sworn to hold the town at all costs. Said Jackson: "This place should be defended with the spirit which actuated the defenders of Thermopylae [a narrow pass in Greece where a few hundred Spartans held out for days against hordes of

Retreating from Patterson's advancing Unionist Army, Jackson's Confederates blow up the Potomac bridge.

Civil War photograph of the ruined Potomac bridge, June 1861.

invading Persians]." But he soon realized that Harpers Ferry could not easily be defended.

Many years before, while trying to sell Congress on Harpers Ferry as a likely sight for an armory, George Washington had described it as "a natural fortress." The nation's most famous military leader was not always right about such things, and Jackson could see that Harpers Ferry was clearly no fortress. It had not one but two Achilles heels, Maryland Heights and Loudoun Heights, each separated from the town by a river. Somewhat like a castle with a moat inside rather than outside its walls, the location made it practically impossible for defenders to hold the vital high ground. Later in the war Jackson would get a chance to hammer this point home to his enemies in blue. "I'd rather take that place fifty times than undertake to defend it once," he said.

When a strong Union force under Gen. Robert Patterson menaced Harpers Ferry from the north and west, the Southerners retreated. Behind them they burned the B & O railroad bridge over the Potomac and the remaining armory buildings, sparing only the small fire engine house, rapidly becoming known as "John Brown's Fort." Later a Confederate raiding party returned to the town and burned the Hall Rifle Factory as well as the covered bridge across the Shenandoah. The conflict, only a few months old, was already exacting a heavy toll on Harpers Ferry.

This war of North against South had placed Harpers Ferry in a very precarious position, smack on the border between the two hostile regions. As Joseph Barry put it, the town was caught "between hawk and buzzard." However, not all of the destruction in Harpers Ferry was the work of soldiers, whether blue-coated or gray. The river junction had become much too dangerous a place for ordinary life and commerce. Many of its citizens had packed up what they could of their belongings, and, depending on their allegiances, fled northward into Maryland, or southward into the heartland of Virginia. Afterwards their abandoned

An artist's depiction of a B & O locomotive and tender thrown from the bridge by the retreating Confederates.

homes became easy prey for looters. As Joseph Barry observed, "it was sad to see the rapid demoralization of the people at this time and the various phases of corrupt human nature suddenly brought to light by the war. Not only were the government buildings ransacked for plunder, but the abandoned houses of the citizens shared the same fate. Even women and children could be encountered at all hours of the day and night loaded with booty or trundling wheelbarrows freighted with all imaginable kinds of portable goods and household furniture. Citizens who recognized their property in the hands of those marauders and claimed it were abused and sometime beaten. . . ."

As the Confederate army marched out of town, local businessman F.A. Roeder felt the need of a modest celebration. So he invited his longtime close friend Joseph Barry into his house for a snort of liquor. Like Barry, Roeder was a stubborn man. No matter how hot things got, he was determined not to flee Harpers Ferry and abandon his home to the looters. "Well, we have got rid of that lot," said Roeder, no doubt pointing southward at the backs of the retreating Confederates. "But what will the next party that comes do with us?"

Not long afterwards, Roeder received a tragic, personal answer to his question. Advancing into Virginia, General Patterson at first ignored Harpers Ferry, but posted part of his Ninth New York Regiment just across the Potomac at Sandy Hook. On July 4, 1861, a raiding party of Union soldiers crossed the Potomac in a small boat, just as Robert Harper had done more than a century before. The object of the raid was the Confederate flag fluttering from the pole at the armory. The New Yorkers pulled down the flag and ripped it into pieces to keep as souvenirs, but they had little time to enjoy their triumph. The clatter of horse's hooves sent them scurrying for their boat as a rear guard Confederate cavalry unit plunged into the town.

Soon, the two sides were flailing away at one another from opposite banks of the Potomac. Because of the distance, the

firing was none too accurate, but the Federals eventually retreated having suffered two of their number killed. The
only casualties on the Southern side were civilians. A man
named Harding, a local shoemaker, had been cut down by a
bullet believed to have been fired by his neighbor, John
Chambers. A fervent Unionist, Chambers had that very day
thrown in his lot with the Northern army.

Late that same afternoon, with the shooting apparently
over, Roeder thought it safe enough for a walk through
town. Across the Potomac was a drunken straggler who had
stumbled onto the scene of the day's battle much too late to
take part in the fighting. Grumbling that he would "kill
some damn rebel anyway," the drunk cut loose with his
musket. His bullet ricocheted off the brick wall of a hotel
and struck Roeder, slicing open his abdomen and depriving
Joseph Barry of yet another friend. Barry saw considerable
irony in the fact that Roeder had been a stout Unionist.

General Patterson's invasion of Virginia proved even
more futile than the July Fourth raid on the burned-out
Harpers Ferry armory, where his troopers had at least
captured a flag. Bamboozled by the outnumbered Confederates, who always seemed to keep several steps ahead of
him, Patterson marched his army around in circles, accom-
plishing little more than to wave his saber in a southerly direction. Eventually, he became convinced that his own army
was outnumbered—actually he held an impressive numeri-
cal superiority of nearly two to one—and fell back on
Harpers Ferry.

Most of Patterson's soldiers put down their muskets and
went home when their three-month term of service was up
about the middle of the summer. Its ranks depleted, the
Union army was then forced to retire across the Potomac
and into Maryland. As they marched away, the Federals
looted the town, taking most of what had been left behind
by the Confederates and non-military thieves. It is said the
retreating bluecoats even stole a tombstone from the Methodist Cemetery.

The seventy-year-old Patterson was himself a "three-month man," and he soon left the army and the war for good—much to the relief of the Federal high command. Patterson's failure to act decisively had proven a very serious matter indeed for the Union cause. With no pressure placed on them by Patterson, the Confederates in the Shenandoah were able to slip away and reinforce their comrades to the east at Manassas. Not far from Manassas, near a creek called Bull Run, Thomas Jackson and some of the men he had drilled and trained at Harpers Ferry stood "like a stone wall" and inflicted the first major defeat on the Union.

Fighting for Bread

For several months after Patterson's departure, Harpers Ferry became a no-man's-land. Neither army felt itself strong enough to hold the town. Rifleman of the 13th Massachusetts Regiment crouched behind rocks and bushes on Maryland Heights firing desultory musket rounds across the river at whatever might be moving. No resident could safely step outdoors or peer through a north-facing window. "It was lucky for the place that they [the Union riflemen] were indifferent marksman," said one citizen who was brave enough to stay. "Else it would have been wholly depopulated." Darkness brought Southern skirmishers who took up positions behind the ruined walls of the armory to fire back at the Northerners and draw still more Union fire down on the town.

On October 16, 1861, the second anniversary of the John Brown raid, the hostilities flared into an all-out battle. More than 20,000 bushels of wheat were stored at Herr's Mill on Virginius Island, and the Union commanders decided to move the grain across the Potomac to make sure it did not end up as bread in the bellies of Confederate soldiers.

Determined to stop the removal and perhaps capture the wheat for his own side, Confederate Col. Turner Ashby marched on Harpers Ferry with 300 infantrymen and 180 cavalrymen. Legend has it that a Harpers Ferry woman swam the Shenandoah to warn Ashby that Northerners had reinforced their positions and now outnumbered him by a dangerous margin. Ashby came on anyway sending his cavalry charging into Bolivar Heights, but the superior numbers of the Federals soon forced him to withdraw.

After a full morning of battle the Federals lost four men. Ashby lost only one man and had his chaplain taken prisoner. Indirect victims of the attack were bakers and bread-hungry families—on the evening following the battle, a small group of Confederate raiders crept onto Virginius Island and burned Herr's mill.

12

"Yankees at Harpers Ferry"

Stonewall in the Valley

Jackson was soon back in the Shenandoah Valley making things miserable for the Union commanders who wanted to claim the region—rich in agricultural produce—for the North. Meanwhile, the Federals used Harpers Ferry as a staging area for repeated advances into the Valley in pursuit of Jackson. Most of these campaigns ended in defeat and retreat for the men in blue.

The Battle of Port Republic illustrates how attempts to trap Jackson and his fast-marching "foot cavalry" typically ended in failure. Charles Frémont, the so-called Pathfinder and unsuccessful Republican presidential candidate in 1856, advanced into the Shenandoah in the spring of 1862 hoping to draw the wily Southern general into a decisive battle. Frémont divided his forces, placing the Union troops under Gen. James Shields across the Shenandoah from his own men at Port Republic. Frémont assumed that, if Jackson attacked either camp, the troops in the other could snatch up their muskets, dash across the bridge at Port Republic, and catch the Confederate general in a vice. It was a clever plan. It might have worked, too, if Jackson's gentlemanly sense of fair play had prevented him from burning the bridge. With the bridge in ashes, Frémont was forced to watch helplessly as Jackson's men mauled Shields.

After Port Republic, the Federal forces along the Shenandoah beat a hasty retreat to Harpers Ferry where they waited for Jackson to swoop down on them out of the Shenandoah. Jackson was no longer in the Valley. He had left his enemies to stand guard over empty fields and marched off to help Robert E. Lee defeat Gen. George McClellan just outside of Richmond. Later in the summer Jackson stood for a second time "like a stone wall" near Manassas. This replay of the Battle of Bull Run ended with the Union army once again retreating in panic toward Washington.

Jackson Returns to the Ferry

Some believe the South might have won the Civil War at the First Battle of Bull Run, but the Confederates were too slow to follow up on their advantage. One year later, on August 30, 1862, when the grays trounced the blues again in the fields outside Manassas, Gen. Robert E. Lee was determined to make proper use of the victory. Having beaten the Union army in a battle only a couple of dozen miles from Washington, Lee decided that the time had come for an invasion of the North. Protected by the Potomac and an iron ring of forts, Washington, D.C., was nearly invulnerable to attack, especially from the south. But Lee thought the city might be successfully approached from the north or west. Consequently, he ordered the Army of Northern Virginia to ford the Potomac just north of Leesburg, a few miles downriver from Harpers Ferry. A band played "Maryland, My Maryland" as the Southern soldiers waded across the river. The Union army, badly shaken at Second Bull Run, did nothing to oppose Lee as he marched northward to Frederick, Maryland. Lee had reason to hope that he could now strike the blow that would end the war, already in its second year.

But Lee made two serious mistakes in military judgment. First he underestimated the time Gen. George McClellan would need to resupply and reinforce the bruised-but-not-defeated Northern army. Lincoln and McClellan had one of the world's most efficient railroad networks on their side and could bring up fresh troops in a hurry, especially when the capital was threatened.

Lee's second mistake was to assume the Northern commander would follow sensible military procedure and evacuate the Harpers Ferry garrison before his army cut off its line of retreat. Lee knew most of the Union generals—McClellan, Meade, Pope, Banks, Burnside, and others; like him, they were all graduates of the war college at West Point. Thus it never occurred to Lee, as he pushed toward Frederick, that his opponents would leave 13,000 of their best troops hopelessly cut off, trapped in fact, at Harpers Ferry. He had assumed the Union garrison would pull back at the first word of his invasion. Lee must have been very much surprised when a scout came riding into his camp in Maryland shouting "Yankees! Yankees at Harpers Ferry."

Those words put an immediate end to any notions Lee might have harbored of threatening Washington or Baltimore. The 13,000 Union soldiers at Harpers Ferry menaced his supply line. So Lee decided to change his objective. If he could not invade the North, then at least he could pick this plum the Union had left hanging behind his line of advance. So he sent Stonewall Jackson marching back toward Virginia—to capture Harpers Ferry.

To accomplish the task Lee had assigned him, Jackson set in motion three columns totalling about 25,000 men. One division under Gen. John Walker took Loudoun Heights, while two divisions under Gen. Lafayette McLaws pushed back the Federal troops holding the crucial high ground of Maryland Heights. With three more divisions under his personal command, Jackson closed in from the south toward Bolivar Heights.

Cannons on the Heights

The defense of Harpers Ferry rested in the hands of Col. Dixon Miles who looked and acted much older than his fifty-eight years. Miles had graduated near the bottom of his class

Col. Dixon Miles, the Harpers Ferry post commander who ordered the surrender of 12,000 Union soldiers pinned down by Stonewall Jackson's artillery. (Photo courtesy of the National Archives)

at West Point, and in thirty-eight years of military service had never managed to distinguish himself in the least. Encircled with enemies, Miles was about to have his chance to rise from the ranks of mediocrity. If he could hold out, even for a few days against the superior numbers of the Confederates, his name would be remembered gloriously.

Miles could hardly have known just how important the coming battle would be. It might very well have brought the war to a close in 1862, and saved the country almost three additional years of bloody fighting. Lee had committed the unpardonable military sin of dividing his forces in enemy territory. What was more, McClellan was well aware that Lee's troops were scattered all over the Maryland and Virginia countryside. In fact, the Union general knew every step the Confederates intended to take—he had a copy of Lee's orders.

When Lee sent Jackson to attack Harpers Ferry, he gave a copy of his plan—Order No. 191—to one of his staff officers who, in turn, used it to wrap the three cigars he had stuffed in his pocket. Later, this extraordinarily negligent officer accidentally dropped both the cigars and the order on the ground. As fate would have it, a Union cavalryman later found the odd bundle, and no doubt, stuck one of the free cigars between his lips. He then rode as hard as he could to McClellan's camp where he presented his commander with a truly priceless piece of military intelligence. Having read the cigar-wrapper order, McClellan swore that he would "whip Bobby Lee with this here piece of paper."

McClellan set out immediately in pursuit of Lee's scattered army. Meanwhile, with Jackson closing in on his position, Miles received a dispatch from headquarters in Washington: "Our army is in motion. It is important that Harper's Ferry be held to the latest moment."

Miles could see that the struggle for Harpers Ferry would be decided on the high ground. If he could hold onto Maryland Heights, then the town might be successfully

Gen. Julius White believed the Union troops at Harpers Ferry should have kept fighting. Although he technically outranked the post commander, White carried out Miles' surrender order after the old colonel was blasted from his horse by an exploding artillery shell. (Photo courtesy of the National Archives)

defended. Otherwise, the enemy would put cannons on the mountains and pound him to pieces with artillery. Miles sent Col. Thomas Ford with five regiments and a squadron of cavalry to the summit and ordered him to hold the mountain "until the cows tails drop off."

At dawn on September 13, a piercing rebel yell rang out from Maryland Heights. McLaws' gray-clad infantry had crept along the spine of the mountain in the night and charged Ford's line at first light. At the center of the Union line was an untried regiment, the 126th New York, its ranks filled with men who had been in the army for only about three weeks. Colonel Ford had feared he could not rely on these raw recruits, but for almost four hours the 126th and their commander, Col. Eliakim Sherill, stood their ground, flinging back one Confederate assault after another. Then disaster struck. A bullet hit Colonel Sherill in the mouth, shattering his teeth and tearing out part of his tongue. A few minutes later, the men of the 126th took to their heels carrying much of Ford's forward line with them. Not all of Ford's troops ran. Several companies of tough veterans tried to force the 126th back into the fight at the point of bayonets.

Ford attempted to form another defensive line about one-quarter mile from his original position, but he had begun to believe he was fighting a losing battle. Soon the panicked Federal soldiers were streaming down the steep slopes of Maryland Heights and hurrying across a pontoon bridge into Harpers Ferry. Retreating artillerymen were spiking the big Union guns that were intended to help them hold the summit and sending them somersaulting down into the Potomac.

An unfortunate army chaplain happened to be standing beside Colonel Miles as he witnessed the disorganized retreat. "God Almighty, what does this mean?" Miles screamed, burning the ears of his chaplain. "They are coming down! Hell and damnation."

Before the end of the day, cheering rebels stood on the crests of both Maryland Heights and Loudoun Heights.

Jackson, who had established communications with Generals McLaws and Walker by means of signal flags, pressed in from the south. The Confederates used up the remainder of September 13 and much of the following morning as well sweating and cursing as they hauled their cannon to the summits of the two mountains. Men had to provide the muscle since horses could not negotiate the steep, rocky slopes. But, by the afternoon of September 14 the Confederate batteries were in place and began to shell Miles's positions in and around Harpers Ferry without mercy.

Meanwhile, the attacking Southerners received the disquieting news that McClellan was advancing toward them from the east with an enormous army, numbering more than 100,000 men. Armed with his cigar wrapper, McClellan was moving with uncharacteristic speed and determination. One prong of McClellan's massive assault had already pushed Lee out of Frederick and was forcing him back toward the Potomac at Sharpsburg. The other prong assailed the mountain passes behind McLaws in an attempt to drive a wedge between Jackson and Lee and lift the siege at Harpers Ferry.

A deadly race was on. Jackson knew he must force Miles to surrender quickly and then hurry off to join forces with Lee at Sharpsburg. Otherwise, McClellan would catch the Confederate army in its current scattered condition and destroy it one piece at a time. Jackson sent a mounted courier to Walker and McLaws with orders to redouble their attack. "Let the work be done thoroughly," he said. "Fire on the houses when necessary. . . . Demolish the place if it is occupied by the enemy and does not surrender."

Miles's batteries on Bolivar Heights and Camp Hill just above the Harpers Ferry Cemetery fought back gamely, often matching the Confederates shell for shell. But as darkness drew its curtain over the second day of the siege, Miles's guns were beginning to run short of ammunition. The Colonel knew he could not hold out for long once his cannons were silenced.

During the night, the Union cavalry commander, Col. Benjamin Davis, concocted a daring scheme. Davis wanted to take the garrison's 1,500 horsemen and try to cut his way out of the encirclement. Miles found himself in such a tight squeeze that cavalry was of little use to him, so he approved Davis's plan. Shortly after midnight, the Federal troopers slipped across the pontoon bridge, lied convincingly to the Southern sentries posted on the Maryland bank of the Potomac, and then rode north. They escaped over the same wagon road John Brown and his raiders had used just three years earlier on their way into Harpers Ferry.

Riding hard for the safety of McClellan's lines, Davis ran smack into a straggling train of Confederate wagons. Having captured or destroyed a quantity of the supplies sorely needed by Lee's army, Davis's men had reason to smile when, at last, they joined up with McClellan's blue legions marching toward Sharpsburg. There were few smiles among the nearly 12,000 Union infantry and artillerymen still trapped at Harpers Ferry.

At dawn on September 15, the Confederate gunners opened up once again. With his artillery almost out of ammunition, Miles summoned his chief subordinates to a desperate council. Some of the Union officers argued against surrender, but a steady downpour of shot and shell rained from the clouds of gunsmoke that hung above the town. "We don't know what to do," Miles said, spreading his hands. "We must surrender."

Having made his decision, Miles sent a rider racing along the summit of Bolivar Heights waving a white flag, and a swelling cheer rose up from the Confederate lines. What Miles did not know was that at the moment he surrendered, McClellan's relief column had reached a point only a few miles east of Harpers Ferry. If he had held on only a few hours more, there would have been no need of surrender, but Miles never learned of this. Their view obscured by smoke and haze, the Confederate batteries on Loudoun Heights had not seen the white flag. One of the last shells fired, before they too received word of the surrender, exploded only a few feet from Colonel Miles, wounding him mortally. A few hours later, lying on a cot at his headquarters in the town, Miles used almost his last breaths to dictate an official report praising certain of his officers and men for their gallantry and willingness to serve where "the danger was thickest." Of his own actions, Miles said "I have done my duty. I am an old soldier and willing to die." Then he did.

It was a ragged Confederate army that marched into Harpers Ferry late in the afternoon of September 15. Their gray uniforms hung on them in tatters, and many were barefoot. Among the most ragged of them was their leader, Stonewall Jackson, who plodded into town on his bedraggled but beloved Old Sorrel. No "fuss and feathers" officer this. Dressed in homespun gray and wearing a broadrimmed hat someone had given him in Martinsburg, Jackson drew cheers not only from his own men but from the Union troops as well. "Boys," said one of the captured Union men, "he isn't much for looks, but if we'd had him, we wouldn't have been caught in this trap."

A Blanket and Two Days' Rations

Jackson had returned to Harpers Ferry, but he did not stay for long. McClellan had finally cornered Lee's vastly outnumbered divisions at Sharpsburg. Just after midnight on the morning of September 16, Jackson and his shoddy, but hard-fighting army set out on the road for Shepherdstown, where they could ford the Potomac and join forces with the main Confederate force under General Lee.

Gen. A.P. Hill and his division remained behind to gather up the captured guns and equipment and parole the Federal prisoners. (The approximately 12,500 men surrendered at Harpers Ferry represented the largest number of American troops captured in any battle up until the fall of Bataan in the Philippines in World War II.) Having signed a parole swearing not to fight against the Confederacy "until properly exchanged," the Union soldiers were set free. They left behind their stacked weapons but were allowed to take with them their blankets and overcoats as well as two days' rations.

The parolees left Harpers Ferry late on the morning of September 16 and trudged toward Annapolis, which lay on the Chesapeake Bay about a hundred miles away. With little more to eat than the two days' rations the Confederates had allowed them, they marched for five days before finally reaching their destination in a thoroughly exhausted, heartsick, and half-starved condition.

In Annapolis, they were afforded no hero's welcome. It would seem that having been surrendered, disarmed, and paroled had somehow sullied them in the eyes of the U.S. Army. Given only two days to recuperate from their ordeal, they were reassigned to fight the Sioux in the west. Only a week after the surrender they found themselves being crammed into cattle cars without water or toilet facilities for a miserable four-day journey by train to Camp Douglas.

Located on land owned by Stephen A. Douglas, the Democratic presidential candidate who had lost to Lincoln in 1860, the camp had previously served as a compound for Confederate war prisoners. The veterans of the battle for Harpers Ferry themselves were being treated almost like POWs—and by their own government. Most were exchanged—for Confederate prisoners paroled by the Union—and returned to regular army service by early the next year, but few forgot the humiliation they had experienced.

While many of the parolees felt shamed by their defeat at Harpers Ferry, they could nevertheless count themselves lucky at having missed the great bloodletting of Antietam that took place just two days after their surrender.

13

The Tide Turns

Death Along Antietam Creek

About seventeen miles to the northwest of Harpers Ferry, a water course called Antietam Creek flows through verdant Maryland countryside and empties into the Potomac. On a series of low hills overlooking the creek, the armies of Robert E. Lee and George McClellan clashed in the bloodiest single day of battle in American history.

Early on the morning of September 16, McClellan's enormous army began to close in on Lee near Sharpsburg. Before Jackson's troops arrived after their mad dash from Harpers Ferry, McClellan held a four-to-one advantage over Lee in numbers, but the always cautious Union general did not attack immediately. Even after Jackson's divisions crossed the river and took up positions on the left of Lee's line, McClellan still outnumbered his foe by almost three-to-one. Still he did not attack.

Lee might have used the day to retreat back across the Potomac fords. Probably he should have, considering the odds he faced. Instead, he held his ground, waiting to see what McClellan would do. Shortly before sunrise on September 17, McClellan showed him.

Gen. Joseph Hooker led his divisions across the fields on the left of Lee's line and hit Jackson's men, who were still exhausted after their forced march from Harpers Ferry. The struggle between Hooker and Jackson surged back and forth through the Maryland countryside, a rumpled quilt stitched from patches of corn, pasture, and woodland. In the end, Jackson held on, though perhaps not like a stone wall.

The next blow came from the same direction and had the same result as the first. Troops under Gen. J.K.F. Mansfield assailed the Confederate left, and Lee blocked them with a division from Texas. Mansfield was shot dead as both sides suffered enormous losses in savage hand-to-hand fighting. The Texans held.

Still more Federal troops marched against the bloodied Southern left. McLaws and Walker, the same Confederate generals who had raked Harpers Ferry with cannon from the summits of Maryland and Loudoun Heights, caught Gen. John Sedgwick's division in an appalling cross fire. In less than thirty minutes the Sedgwick division was all but wiped out, and more than 2,000 of its blue-coated warriors lay dead or writhing in agony in a wooded area just north of Sharpsburg.

Much of the carnage of the battle was produced by cannon. More than five hundred artillery pieces were used at Antietam, a substantial majority of them by McClellan's huge army. At one point in the battle, General Hooker's sharp eyes caught the glint of morning sunlight on the bayonets of a Southern unit deployed in a large cornfield. He ordered his artillerymen to harvest the field. Hooker described the scene: "Every stalk of corn in the northern and greater part of the field was cut as closely as could have been done with a knife, and the slain lay in rows precisely as they had stood in their ranks a few moments before. It was never my fortune to witness a more bloody, dismal battlefield."

Late in the morning, the Union attack shifted to the center of the Southern line, where thousands of gray-clad infantrymen stood in a country road which had been cut down into the Maryland clay. Before the fighting was over, the sunken road would be piled high with Confederate dead. Forever after, the road would be known as "Bloody Lane." But although Lee's center wavered and seemed ready to crumble, it held.

All morning McClellan had urged General Burnside to throw his divisions into the battle and attack the Confederate right. But Burnside complained that he could not get his troops across a key bridge over Antietam Creek—known to most now as the "Burnside Bridge." A few hundred Georgia riflemen scattered along a hillside overlooking the creek had fought off one Yankee charge after another, clogging the bridge with blue-clad bodies. Apparently, it had not occurred to Burnside to simply have his men wade across the creek.

Finally one of Burnside's divisions marched south of the bridge and forded the creek. At about one in the afternoon they struck the Southern defenders from the side, driving them back toward Sharpsburg at a run. Lee's line was collapsing. Unless he could stop the Union attack rolling in over the fields to his right, the Army of Northern Virginia would be destroyed and with it, almost certainly, the Confederacy. At just this critical moment, an ear-splitting rebel yell caused soldiers in both the grappling armies to suck in their breath. It came from the direction of Harpers Ferry.

A.P. Hill's division had left the river junction early that morning. Some of the captured war material still had not been loaded onto wagons and some Federal prisoners remained to be paroled, but Hill and his men knew they were urgently needed at Sharpsburg, from which direction guns could already be heard booming. All morning and into the afternoon they marched, fording the Potomac near Shepherdstown and approaching the right wing of Lee's army at just the moment the Confederate line was breaking.

In front of Hill, Union troops swarmed across the fields in pursuit of retreating Southerners. Without a moment's hesitation, Hill, dressed in his red battle shirt, raised his sword and gave the order to charge. The counterattack caught the Federals completely by surprise, and soon they themselves were reeling back in a disorderly retreat.

The Battle of Antietam was over. Soldiers on both sides fell to the ground in exhaustion from the all-day struggle. Many turned their faces away in horror at the ghastly scene before them. The carnage stretched for more than three miles across the grassy hills and shallow valleys on either side of Sharpsburg. More than 23,000 men had been killed, wounded or reported missing. No foreign enemy has ever struck down that many Americans in a single day of combat.

For what remained of the afternoon and all of the following day the two armies faced one another like wounded and wary lions. McClellan had a tremendous advantage in numbers, guns, and munitions. He might have decisively defeated Lee if he had renewed the struggle on the second day. But he did not. Probably McClellan was too shaken by the magnitude of the slaughter to fight any more on those bloodied fields.

Antietam changed the way many Americans perceived the war; certainly the battle deeply moved the men who had fought in it. Instead of a high-spirited affair filled with pomp and polished brass and dashing young men in fine uniforms, the war would now be seen more for what it really was—the dark, bloody, and methodical business of killing.

On the second night after the battle, General Lee ordered his men to bank their campfires to deceive their enemies and then slip across the Potomac fords. No doubt, most of Lee's soldiers who returned to Virginia that night considered themselves quite lucky to have survived Antietam. Ironically, more of these men might have lived to see the end of the war if A.P. Hill's division had not arrived just in time to save the day for Lee. If McClellan had forced Lee to surrender at Antietam, the war would have ended quickly. As it was, the fighting dragged on for almost three more years. The Army of Northern Virginia fought the Army of the Potomac again and again and there were many more fields littered with the bodies of men whose chief difference of opinion was over their choice of color in uniforms.

Black soldiers at Harpers Ferry. (Courtesy of U.S. Signal Corps, photo #111-BA-1829, in the National Archives)

Civil War era artist's conception of the Union Army camp at Harpers Ferry.

Abraham Lincoln Visits the Ferry

With the Confederates in retreat, McClellan moved his headquarters to Harpers Ferry. Most of the town's citizens had long ago given up the place and taken their lives and families elsewhere. Those few hardy souls who remained saw countless campfires light up the hills above the rivers at night. One resident imagined that the Trojans must have seen a similar sight 3,000 years earlier when the Greek army camped beneath their walls.

About a week after the Battle of Antietam, Abraham Lincoln issued the Emancipation Proclamation, which would take effect on January 1, 1863, and thus accomplish by law what John Brown had hoped to accomplish with rifles. Had he lived to see it, Brown probably would have denounced the Proclamation as too weak—it only freed slaves in those Southern states that refused to make peace with the North.

A few days after signing the Proclamation, the president paid McClellan a visit at his new headquarters. Looking even taller, thinner, and bonier than usual, Lincoln explored the streets of Harpers Ferry dressed in his famous chimney-pot hat and black frock coat. He walked through the burned-out armory, tarrying at the little fire engine house to consider the importance of the stand John Brown had made there just under three years before. Many thousands of Americans had died in battle since that fateful night when Brown and his raiders brought their Sharps rifles to Harpers Ferry. It must have pained Lincoln to think that many thousands more of his countrymen would not live to see the nation once more at peace.

While pondering the tragic results of the Harpers Ferry raid, Lincoln may very well have heard his troops singing a new version of the "Battle Hymn of the Republic." In place of the usual words, they substituted "John Brown's body lies a'moldering in the grave. . . . He's gone to be a soldier in the army of the Lord. . . . His soul's marching on."

Hoping to see the conflict ended as quickly as possible,

Lincoln urged McClellan to pursue the Confederates until he could force Lee to fight a decisive battle. Instead, McClellan dallied in Harpers Ferry, fortifying the heights surrounding the town and repairing the bridges blown up by the retreating Southerners. When, after two months, McClellan finally did set out in search of his foe, he ambled southward, covering only about six miles a day.

"He's an admirable engineer," Lincoln said of his over-cautious general. "But he seems to have a special talent for a stationary engine."

Frustrated by McClellan's sluggish leadership, Lincoln placed Ambrose Burnside in command of the Army of the Potomac. Burnside moved faster than McClellan, but he crossed one bridge too many in Virginia and was soundly beaten on the banks of the Rappahannock. Joseph Hooker then stepped into what was rapidly becoming a revolving door command.

On the Way to Gettysburg

Among those who would not live to witness the fulfillment of Lincoln's dream of a nation at peace was Stonewall Jackson. In the early summer of 1863, the old, ragged warrior was accidentally cut down by his own men who were in the process of defeating the Union army at Chancellorsville. He would be remembered—and sorely missed—by the men in gray when they passed by Harpers Ferry a few weeks later.

Having soundly whipped his enemies at Chancellorsville, Lee once more brought his army to the Potomac fords at Shepherdstown. Three Confederate corps, numbering about 20,000 men each, slogged across the river and over the Antietam battlefield, so thoroughly bloodied just nine months earlier. In a few days time, they would participate in the bloodying of a similar collection of grassy fields—just outside Gettysburg in Pennsylvania.

Meanwhile, the Union army had yet another change of command. With Lee headed north, Hooker determined not to make the mistake of leaving an isolated garrison at Harpers Ferry. Hooker's decision to abandon the town angered Lincoln's War Department and cost him his job. McClellan had been fired because he was in no hurry to leave Harpers Ferry, and now, ironically, Hooker was sacked because he refused to stay.

Gen. George Meade was next in line for the revolving door, and he hurried his army to Pennsylvania to block the Confederates' path at Gettysburg. On July 1, the Southerners attacked. Meade's skill as a commander was probably no greater than that of his predecessors, but this fight differed markedly from earlier Civil War battles. This time it was the Union soldiers who had their homes at their backs. Among the thousands of blue-clad soldiers arrayed on the hills above the town were many of the same men whose units had fought and been dishonored (in the eyes of their fellow soldiers) at Harpers Ferry during the Antietam campaign. But this time they clung stubbornly to the high ground, and in the face of Pickett's charge, one of history's most murderous frontal assaults, they stood unyielding—like a stone wall.

A Vote for West Virginia

Soundly defeated, Lee's army retreated from the North the way it had come, across the Potomac fords above Harpers Ferry. By their own reckoning, the Confederates were now back on home ground in Virginia. From the viewpoint of the Union, Lee's divisions were still in enemy territory. The way Northerners saw it, Harpers Ferry and Shepherdstown were no longer part of Virginia. A few weeks earlier, this part of the Old Dominion had voted itself out of Virginia and into the newly formed state of West Virginia.

Even today there are those who say that Jefferson County rightfully belongs in Virginia, not West Virginia. In favor of their argument they have at least one telling point: the vote in Jefferson County was almost certainly fixed. Balloting, which took place under the watchful eyes of the occupying Union forces, yielded a vote of 248-2 in favor of joining West Virginia.

This lopsided result could hardly have represented the true sentiments of the county's citizens. It is absurd to imagine that less than one percent of the voters wished their county to remain part of Virginia. In truth, the West Virginia issue was never really decided at the polls, but rather on the battlefield.

Col. George Armstrong Custer riding past the armory engine house in August of 1864. Twelve years later Custer would keep an appointment with destiny on Montana's Little Bighorn River. (Photo courtesy of HFNHP. Credit: Western Reserve Historical Society, Cleveland, Ohio)

14

The Final Curtain

Early's Race to Washington

Following Lee's calamitous defeat at Gettysburg, the military fortunes of the Confederacy fell into steady decline. Command of the Northern army, which for three years had passed like a bad cold from one blue-coated general to the next, settled at last onto the capable shoulders of Ulysses S. Grant, a much faster-moving and more determined leader than any the Union had seen before. Grant soon had the Southern army tied down defending Richmond, and with Lee unable to maneuver, the Confederacy was left with little possibility of victory. Still the men of the South continued to believe that with some bold stroke they might turn the tide in their favor. For a few brief weeks in the summer of 1864, that hope almost became a reality.

In June of that year, a powerful Federal force under the ruthless command of Gen. David ("Black Dave") Hunter ran loose in the strategic Shenandoah Valley. Although the son of a prominent Virginia planter, Hunter was a zealous abolitionist and ardent Unionist as well as a personal acquaintance of President Lincoln. To Hunter, the suppression of John Brown's raid at Harpers Ferry was an evil of such magnitude that it justified the total destruction of Virginia. Brown's "moldering" body cried out for revenge, and in the Valley Hunter and his men were meting it out, burning homes, trampling crops, and slaughtering livestock.

To stop Hunter's pillaging, Lee sent Gen. Jubal Early into the Valley with an army of 14,000 tough veterans. Rough in appearance, speech, and manners, Early reminded many of the late Stonewall Jackson. And just as Jackson might have done, Early caught the marauding Federals completely by surprise, throwing them into headlong retreat and driving them westward, out of the Valley and deep into the Allegheny Mountains.

Suddenly, with Hunter out the way, the road north lay open. Early shared another characteristic with Jackson— audacity. With Washington, D.C., only a few days' march from the Valley, the Confederate general decided to take a desperate gamble. Hurrying to the Potomac fords, he aimed to cross the river, cut to the east, and storm into the capital before Lincoln could muster a defense. Grant's Army of the Potomac was dug in around Richmond, the Confederate capital, almost a hundred miles south of Washington. In fact, the only Federal force of any size between Early and the steps of the White House was a relatively small garrison of six regiments at Harpers Ferry.

By 1864, field officers on both sides of the war had learned the hard lesson that Harpers Ferry was a trap and had given up trying to defend it. Usually they abandoned the place long before their pickets sighted the first enemy sabers. The commander of the Union garrison, the German-born Gen. Max Weber, was well aware of Harpers Ferry's weaknesses as a defensive position. His superiors in Washington sent Weber a blunt telegram threatening to hang "the first man who proposes a surrender or retreat." But faced with the alternative of being hopelessly snared in the town as Miles had been, Weber chose to take his chances with the hangman's noose. He evacuated Harpers Ferry and took up a strong position on Maryland Heights.

History would show that Weber had made a wise decision. Early pushed into Harpers Ferry on July 3 and wasted valuable time trying to dislodge Weber from the Heights. He did not succeed, and on July 6, he gave up the effort and rushed on toward Washington. It took the mostly barefoot Confederate soldiers three more days to trudge through the mountain passes of central Maryland. Meanwhile, Lincoln fired off a wire to General Grant pleading for troops to defend the capital. Grant started loading men into railroad boxcars.

Time was already running out on the Confederates when, on July 9, they swept aside a small Union force, which had been hastily deployed along the banks of the Monocacy River. Two days later the invaders reached the network of forts and trenches encircling Washington. Early had hoped to the end that he would find the capital fortifications weak and lightly manned. Instead, when Early caught his first glimpse of the Capitol dome, he also saw line after blue line of seasoned Federal infantrymen arrayed in the forts and trenches between him and his objective. Had he arrived only a few hours before, his men might have walked right over the Union trenches, straight down Pennsylvania Avenue, and right up the steps of the Capitol building itself. But not now. Thousands of Union troops had arrived in Washington by boat and train that same morning. It was all too clear to the Confederates that delay had dealt their bold plan a fatal blow. General Early was late.

Sheridan on the March

Time was running out on the Confederacy. Early retreated back across the Potomac and down into Virginia, and after that, Harpers Ferry was never again seriously threatened by a Confederate army.

Still the town at the river forks continued to play a major role in the war. It became a giant storehouse for rifles and "Minie Balls," cannon and shells, wagons and horses. Gen. Philip Sheridan made Harpers Ferry his depot for stockpiling the mountains of war material needed for his extensive campaigns in the Shenandoah Valley.

Like Grant, Sheridan was a new breed of Union commander. Grim, pugnacious, and tireless, he shrugged off defeat on one battlefield after another, always pushing on quickly to the next engagement with the enemy and always moving the Union one step closer to victory. Earlier in 1864, Sheridan had led a huge cavalry raid that took him almost to the gates of Richmond. The raid ended in retreat for the Union horsemen, but they accomplished one very important objective—they killed the Confederacy's swashbuckling cavalry leader, J.E.B. Stuart. The man who had faced John Brown eye-to-eye at the armory engine house was dead, and the Union commander who killed him made his headquarters at Harpers Ferry within sight of the armory ruins.

In the Shenandoah, Sheridan's strategy was simple: to use his vast superiority in numbers and supplies to overwhelm his opponents. The orders Grant gave Sheridan were just as simple: "Wherever the enemy goes let our troops go also."

At first Sheridan moved cautiously, falling back on Harpers Ferry so often that his men nicknamed their leader "Harpers Weekly." But soon the heavy weight of the Federal army's superior numbers began to take its toll. Sheridan routed Early's troops at Winchester. Then when the outnumbered Confederates tried to strike back with a surprise attack at Cedar Creek, Sheridan whipped them so soundly that he was able to drive Early completely out of the Shenandoah Valley.

Like Gen. William Tecumseh Sherman, who turned portions of Georgia and the Carolinas into a wasteland, Sheridan fought not so much to win battles, but to win the war. Determined to make the Valley useless to the Confederates, he destroyed crops, slaughtered livestock, burned barns, houses, and entire towns. Just as John Brown did in Kansas and at Harpers Ferry, Sheridan made war on civilians.

Sometimes the people fought back. When a group of Union soldiers manhandled a Harpers Ferry girl, the young woman's mother exacted a gruesome revenge. She invited the

Gen. Philip Sheridan's headquarters in a commandeered Harpers Ferry residence.

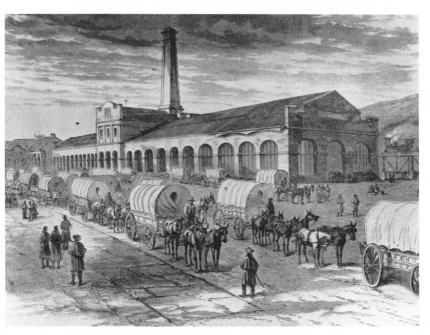

Teamsters line up their wagons to keep a river of supplies moving south to Sheridan's victorious army.

troopers to enjoy an apple pie which she had apparently laced with arsenic. Several of the soldiers died in convulsions.

Trapping a Gray Fox

As the Confederate army retreated southward, the war in the Shenandoah was carried on by guerilla bands that continued the fight behind enemy lines. Striking from his lair deep in the Blue Ridge Mountains, Col. John Mosby's Rangers carried out lightning raids on vulnerable Union positions, stealing supplies, blowing up ammunition dumps, and derailing B & O trains. In one famous incident, Mosby swooped down on one of Sheridan's supply trains outside Berryville and made off with more than seventy wagons heavy with food and munitions.

Along with Mosby rode his friend and trusted associate, young Capt. John Mobley of Harpers Ferry. The similarity of the two men's names generated almost as much confusion in Northern newspapers as the Rangers themselves created among their enemies. The two often led separate bands striking simultaneously at targets in widely separated parts of the Valley. To the Northerners it seemed that Mosby, Mobley—or whatever his name was—was everywhere.

Only a few years before, at the time of the John Brown raid, Mobley had been a teenaged loafer idling away his hours on the streets of Harpers Ferry. The boy was so shiftless that he was often the butt of jokes aimed at him by adults or his harder-working peers. It is said Mobley laughed right along with those who made fun of him. But something about the war, perhaps the burning homes, the death of a friend, or the adventure of it all, put fire in the boy.

In time, Mobley, who had once been the butt of jokes, became a rough-riding adventurer and seasoned killer, the toughest of the Confederate raiders. Usually operating as leader of his own, small band of guerrillas, Mobley cut telegraph wires and hit isolated Union outposts. Often, when he captured food or clothing from his Northern enemies, he shared them with the hungry and homeless. The wretched

A Confederate commando, young John Mobley of Harpers
Ferry was much feared and hated by the Union command.
Late in the war, Mobley was betrayed by a friend and killed
in an ambush. (Photo courtesy of HFNHP. Credit:
Helen Cooke, Leesburg, Virginia)

farmers of the Shenandoah Valley, impoverished by the marches of Hunter and Sheridan, looked upon Mobley as a hero. Legends sprang up around him like those that celebrate Jesse James, who incidentally, was himself a Confederate partisan.

To the Northerners, however, Mobley was no hero. Rather, Federal commanders who struggled to keep the trains running and their supply wagons safe, regarded him as a murderer and thief. Indeed, as Confederate fortunes waned and the war entered its closing months, Mobley lived less the life of an adventuring ranger and more that of a fugitive outlaw. His band of followers dwindled to fifteen, then to four, then to none. On several occasions his enemies had the young raider practically in their grasp only to have him slip away and disappear like a puff of smoke in the wind.

One day in February of 1865, during the Confederacy's last and coldest winter, a Union cavalry unit discovered Mobley's headquarters in the tiny community of Snickers Gap in Virginia's Loudoun County. The soldiers searched house after house but could not find the raider. He had eluded them and fled over the heavy snow in a sleigh. That night, the troopers overtook Mobley's sleigh. With the blue-capped riders almost upon him, Mobley jumped out of his sleigh, severed the harnesses with a single sweep of his saber, and galloped to safety on one of the horses.

Luck was running out for Mobley just as it was for the Confederacy. For a $1000 bribe, a supposed friend lured Mobley into an ambush. The unsuspecting raider rode confidently along a mountain trail to a prearranged rendezvous. Mobley's friend was not there. Without warning, rifles blazed away from the trees on either side, riddling Mobley with bullets. Later in the day, April 5, 1865, the victorious ambushers dumped Mobley's bloody body into the dust on Shenandoah Street in Harpers Ferry. Mobley had not yet reached his twenty-first birthday.

Four days after Mobley was cut down, Lee surrendered at Appomattox.

The Last Act

News of Lee's surrender sent joyous throngs pouring through the streets of Washington. An enormous crowd gathered around a band on the White House lawn to serenade President Lincoln with patriotic songs. Surprisingly, Lincoln asked the band to play "Dixie," the Daniel Emmett minstrel tune that had become something of a national anthem for the now defeated Confederacy. Some in the crowd cried out angrily when they recognized the tune, but their boos quickly turned to cheers. It was an important and symbolic moment. With the war won, Lincoln hoped to knit the nation back together and heal its grievous wounds as quickly as possible. He would never get the chance.

Less than a week after Appomattox, Lincoln joined his wife, Mary Todd, in a box at Ford's Theatre to enjoy a performance of "Our American Cousin." During the third act, John Wilkes Booth stepped quietly through the door behind the presidential party, put a pistol to the back of Lincoln's head, and pulled the trigger.

Having witnessed the hanging of John Brown in Charles Town, Booth had been in on the beginning of the war. Now he fired its last shot.

Almost miraculously, Booth escaped Washington and rode hard, some would say, for Harpers Ferry, where his wife awaited him. But Booth never reached the Ferry. Trapped, he died in a blazing barn in Virginia, his body burned beyond recognition.

Five and a half years had passed since John Brown had proclaimed his gospel of violence in Harpers Ferry. Ironically, standing in the door of a fire house, he had set fire to a nation, and more than 600,000 Americans had been consumed in the flames of war. Among the dead were most of the men who had been touched directly by Brown's electrifying raid of the U.S. armory and arsenal: Brown himself, tried, convicted, and hanged; eighteen of the brave men who had accompanied Brown on that fateful night, shot, cut down by sabers, or hanged along with Brown at Charles Town; J.E.B. Stuart, who fell in a desperate stand with his horsemen outside of Richmond; Stonewall Jackson, shot accidentally by his own men; Mobley, the ranger, shot from ambush; President Lincoln, shot in the midst of a play, a comedy; Booth, his assassin, in a flaming barn in Virginia. Even Robert E. Lee, in a very real sense, gave up his life to the war. When Lee, who had stood on the armory grounds in Harpers Ferry and demanded John Brown's surrender, was forced at last to surrender his own comrades-in-arms to Ulysses S. Grant, he told his weary generals: "I would rather die a thousand deaths."

15

Wounded But Not Dead

The Ruins of War

Among the casualties of America's most tragic conflict was the little town where the war between brothers had begun. During four bloody years of fighting, the blues and the grays traded Harpers Ferry back and forth, shelling it as they attacked and burning it as they retreated. Most of the town's residents had fled from the cannons of the Sheridans, Jacksons, Earlys, and Hunters. When the fighting finally ended, people drifted back to find their former homes, mills, and factories in utter ruin. All but a few of the returnees were too poor or too disheartened to start over— at least in this place. So Harpers Ferry never fully recovered from the beating it took in the Civil War.

The War Department decided firmly against rebuilding the armory. The fire-blackened walls crumbled, and although water still flowed through the armory millrace, it no longer turned wheels or raised trip-hammers. Instead, it fed a swamp. Eventually the armory land was sold to the B & O and other private concerns.

Time and again, enterprising men tried to harness the power of the rivers and start up new factories at Harpers Ferry. Just when an industry seemed firmly established, one or both of the rivers would rise up and knock it down.

Even in this century the flood problem has not abated. The 1936 flood, shown above, brought water up to ceiling level.

The destruction begun by invading Civil War armies was continued by the rivers. Above, an 1889 flood has made a shambles of Shenandoah Street.

So much timber had been cut along the banks of the Potomac and Shenandoah, much of it during the war, that the river valleys had lost all resistance to flood. In 1870, the same raging crest that carried the eccentric inventor Wernwag downriver on the roof of his house, also swept away half of Harpers Ferry's houses and businesses. Afterwards, major floods hit the town every ten to fifteen years.

But the town hung on. Although wounded by the war and constantly punished by its rivers, Harpers Ferry did not die. Its people, impoverished and reduced to a fraction of their previous numbers, clung to their homes and made their living as best they could. When the floods came, they took to high ground. When the waters retreated, they slogged back through the sticky mud, and as Robert Harper had done so often before them, pulled out their tools and set to patching things up.

The Quiet Poet of Harper's Ferry

Among those who time and again helped clean up and dry out the town after the rivers had their way with it was a watchman, tinker, and schoolteacher by the name of Joseph Barry. To live at the junction of the Potomac and Shenandoah has always required a broad streak of tenacity as well as a good sense of humor. Barry, who along with the town, survived countless floods, fires, shellings, and invasions, possessed a healthy portion of both those qualities.

At one time or another, every village has its poet. Barry was the poet of Harpers Ferry. None of Barry's poems were ever published, and that is probably just as well. Most of them are love sonnets which, as a youth, he composed by the dozen in praise of the young Harpers Ferry women he courted with enthusiasm but without much success.

Born sometime before 1840, Barry lived right up into the twentieth century and saw the arrival of a whole new era, and before he died, he gave the world something far more valuable and entertaining than his poems—a history of Harpers Ferry as seen with his own eyes. A sensitive, quiet,

Only a scattering of burned-out buildings and the engine house remain in this photograph taken after the Civil War. Eventually, all traces of the armory, including the "John Brown Fort," would be removed from the property.

A 19th-century view of High Street.

and observant man, Barry had witnessed first hand the John Brown raid, had seen Jackson on Old Sorrel and Sheridan on his charger. So, late in his life, Barry took a pencil in his hand and wrote it all down—the floods, the fires, the fist fights, the petty arguments, and the artillery duels.

Of the John Brown incident, Barry's chief memory was his own mad, zigzag scramble up a steep alley with bullets zinging after him. Later, his friends made light of his adventure, maintaining that Barry was so thin, the raiders had no real hope of finding him with a musket ball. But Barry knew the real reason he had reached safety. As he ran, a slave named Hannah, the servant and cook of one of Barry's neighbors, dashed out into the alley and spread her arms so that the raiders could not fire without fear of hitting her.

Barry was not a land-owning aristocrat and had no need of servants either black or white. Since he owed his life to Hannah's quick thinking and bravery, it is, perhaps, not surprising that he confessed no love of slavery. But, like all of Barry's opinions, his opposition to slavery was not of the radical sort, and when the Civil War broke out, he refused to wear the uniform of either Union or Confederacy. "Personally," he said, "we owe too little to either party to take sides very decidedly."

In his book, Barry pokes fun at some of the men who did choose to fight their fellow Americans. He tells how a group of Union men used a stack of live artillery shells as a platform for their camp fire. "Soon a terrific explosion shook the surrounding hills," said Barry, "sending all the culinary utensils flying over the tree tops."

Barry tells of a foot-weary platoon of western conscripts who, ignorant of the dangerous grades on some eastern railroads, decided to use a parked railroad boxcar as an easy conveyance down a steep incline. Harpers Ferry folk were astonished as the boxcar "shot like a meteor" through town "and the long hair of the western men streamed behind." Fortunately, no one either on or off the car was killed in the

incident, but when the car finally rolled to a stop, a furious
Union officer had the terrified riders clamped in irons for
being lazy and stupid.

Barry also tells how a group of Confederate stragglers,
hiding in a Harpers Ferry smithy, sent one of their number
out to spy on the Federal troops who had just overrun the
town. The scout was a local man, a German immigrant who
spoke with a thick accent. Known to his neighbors as "Dutch
George," he was not thought of as a particularly clever fellow. In fact, the Yankees easily outsmarted Dutch George
and captured him. "By damn," said George to his captors,
"You did dat wery vel, but you ain'ty schmart enough to find
de boys in de blackschmidt shop."

Perhaps it is understandable that, generally speaking,
Barry had a low opinion of the soldiers. He had watched
them burn and loot private businesses, put people out of
their homes, commandeer wagons, horses, and food, and
shell the town indiscriminately from the surrounding
heights. "An undisciplined, armed rabble," he called them,
"for candor obliges us thus designate both the armies en-
gaged in this war."

So the heroes of Barry's book are not soldiers. Instead
they are women like Hannah and men such as the pre-war
armory superintendent Col. Edward Lucas who, it is said,
never fired an employee. Instead, when faced with a recal-
citrant worker, Lucas would drag the man out into the
street and, according to Barry, "administer a sound
thrashing."

Despite his toughness, Colonel Lucas was apparently a
good-hearted man. Old and worn-out slaves in the area often appealed to Lucas to save them from being "sold down
the river" into a harsher existence on some plantation in the
deep South. Whenever he could, Lucas would buy the slave,
and "consequently," noted Barry, "he always had the most
useless lot of servants in Virginia."

Lucas's favorite servant was a lean and sinewy little man
named Tanner who loved to fight almost as much as did his

master. "One day," said Barry, "Tanner had a fight with another negro and, while they were belaboring one another, the Colonel happened to come up, and, seeing his servant in a tight place, he called out, 'Pitch in Tanner! Pitch in Tanner!' The street arabs took up the cry, and it has been used ever since at Harpers Ferry in cases where great exertion of muscle or energy is recommended."

It is easy to imagine Barry and his neighbors calling out "Pitch in Tanner!" as they struggled to put the town right after the war. Without the help of former slaves they would likely never have succeeded. Many of the hands that cleared rubble, drove nails, or laid brick were those of young black men and women who, following the war, flocked to Harpers Ferry. The freed slaves John Brown and his raiders had watched for in vain, had finally arrived. However, they came not to fight, but to get an education.

The engine house after it was reconstructed on the Storer campus. (Photo courtesy of Bruce Roberts)

JOHN BROWN
AT HARPERS FERRY

Prof. Henry T. McDonald, President Storer College

Harpers Ferry, W. Va., will Lecture at the

Town Hall, Fairmount Heights, Md.

Friday, April 25, 1913, 8 P. M.

ADMISSION - - 10 CENTS

Concerned citizens and Storer College officials raised money to return the engine house/fort to Harpers Ferry.

16

Reflection of the Past

The Truth Shall Make You Free

The dust kicked up by the marching armies had barely settled when it became apparent that with all its bloodshed and destruction the Civil War had purchased very little true freedom for the slaves of the South. Despite the Emancipation Proclamation and the defeat of the Confederacy, most of America's black people remained locked in chains of ignorance and poverty.

Believing education could succeed where violence had failed, a young and idealistic New England minister named Nathan Brackett moved to Harpers Ferry. With money from John Storer, a wealthy friend in his native Maine, Brackett founded Storer College, a school for the sons and daughters of former slaves. Placing emphasis on the practical, the college taught sewing, cooking, gardening, blacksmithing, drafting, and carpentry—the very skills its students would need to survive as free people. Built by the students themselves, the wood and brick college buildings rose one after another on the hill behind Harpers Ferry. Eventually the Storer campus dominated the hilltop where both Union and Confederate armies had camped and where General Miles had made his fatal stand against Jackson's encircling army.

In time, Storer evolved into a kind of prep school and was known as one of the very best educational facilities for blacks in America. As its reputation grew, Storer officials boasted that their school's "isolation from the little town and all outside society renders it especially favorable for study." To maintain this "favorable" atmosphere for learning, school authorities discouraged all contact with the town of Harpers Ferry with its seductive stores, theaters, and saloons. Students were required to maintain proper academic decorum at all times. "Students are presumed to be ladies and gentlemen," said one Storer catalogue, "and can remain connected with the school only so long as the presumption is maintained." The school prohibited "liquor, smoking, profanity, card playing, jump dancing, or throwing slops from any of the windows." Young ladies could not "visit the railroad station, leave the grounds at night . . . or appear in public . . . expensively or showily dressed."

Storer catalogues encouraged "simple dress," especially for female students. "Velvet and velvetine in the schoolroom are costly and objectionable. . . . a simple school dress . . . consists of a plaited woolen skirt attached to . . . an elastic Jersey bodice. Such a dress, worn with one underskirt and two layers of underclothing—one pure wool, the other cotton—solves the school problem; and a corded corset waist to which the stocking suspenders are attached supplies the continuation to one underskirt and really outlines without compressing the figure."

The school's 1916 catalogue suggested students bring with them the following list of items: "Your Bible, a toothbrush, three towels, brush and comb, three table napkins, umbrella, bedding if you do not wish to hire it." Of course, students in later years also needed to bring a little money, but only very little. The catalogue reminded young scholars that "an entrance fee of 50 cents is required from each student." Rent for a private room with a stove, double bedstead, table, and chair would cost $2 for three months or $3 for a full eight-month term. The catalogue recommended a monthly budget of $7 for board, $1.50 for rent and tuition, $1 for washing, and $.50 for fuel. It was also pointed out that "students can afford to economize on almost anything better than books. For first supply, from $2 to $5 should be brought."

Of course, books were only one part of a student's Storer experience. The place itself was an education. From the doorways of their lecture halls and workshops the Storer students looked out on the view that Thomas Jefferson (several of Brackett's early students claimed to be descended from Jefferson) had praised as "worth a trip across the Atlantic." They also looked down on the armory fire engine house, where John Brown and his raiders had held on desperately waiting in vain for slaves to run to him and fill up the ranks of his hopelessly outnumbered army.

A Mirror Image

The only armory building that survived the constant shelling and burning was the fire engine house where John Brown had made his last stand. After the war, the little, decaying building attracted droves of curious visitors who came to Harpers Ferry looking for traces of its violent past. For decades enterprising Harpers Ferry youngsters made apple and licorice money by selling bricks from "John Brown's Fort" to gullible travelers on B & O trains. It is said they sold enough bricks to construct dozens of buildings the size of the engine house.

In 1893, a group of investors decided they could outdo the town's barefoot children; they had the engine house dismantled and shipped by rail to the Chicago Exposition where it was reassembled as a sideshow exhibit. Unhappily for backers of the scheme, John Brown's Fort was assigned to a far corner of the Exposition grounds, and hardly any tickets were sold. In fact, the fort was such a flop at the fair that investors went bust and had to leave the building on a Chicago rail siding.

After several years, a group of concerned citizens, who

The engine house/fort before it was pulled down and shipped to Chicago as an exhibit. (Photo courtesy of B & O Railroad)

could not bear to see the pile of historic bricks and lumber forever abandoned, raised the money to bring the little edifice back home. But not everybody in Harpers Ferry was glad to see the old structure again. Most of the town's residents were all too well aware that it attracted an endless stream of troublesome visitors who never ran out of annoying questions. None of the town's property owners would have the dismantled engine house on their land, so it ended up in a barn on a farm about two miles from Harpers Ferry.

In 1906, author and educator W.E.B. Du Bois led a group of black preachers and professors on a pilgrimage to the barn. Du Bois' followers, all of them members of his Niagara Movement, had been meeting at Storer College to discuss ways of winning broader freedoms for blacks in America—the dreams of men such as John Brown and Frederick Douglass had still not been realized. Feeling they were on sacred ground, some of the visitors took off their shoes and approached the barn in bare feet. Heaven knows what they stepped in, and all they saw was a stack of rotting boards and battered bricks, but the experience touched them deeply. Within three years, Du Bois and his associates helped found the National Association for the Advancement of Colored People, which would be pivotal in the American civil rights movement. The key event in that movement was the winning of a school desegregation case in Kansas. The victorious litigant was a child named Brown.

Eventually, the students at Storer got possession of John Brown's Fort, the engine house, and brought it to their campus. Working from an old photographic negative, they lovingly restored the structure brick by brick. But because the negative was a mirror image, the features of the building were reversed.

Things often get turned around backwards at Harpers Ferry—even dreams. For almost ninety years Storer College offered a sound education to former slaves, their children, grandchildren, and great-grandchildren. Storer graduates went on to win places of eminence in an American society still

Members of the National League of Colored Women visiting the John Brown Fort in 1896.

Members of the Niagara Movement at Harpers Ferry in 1906: (seated) W. E. B. DuBois; (standing left to right) J. R. Clifford, L. M. Hershaw, and F. H. M. Murray.

not at ease with notions of racial equality. Some of them returned to Harpers Ferry, bought homes, and themselves taught classes at Storer. But the college, which functioned mostly as a high school, was forced to close its doors in 1955. Ironically, Storer fell victim to the very forces of racial justice that had been so often advocated on its campus. The integration of Virginia and West Virginia schools, following the Supreme Court decision in the Brown case, drew so many students away from Storer that the school finally had to shut down.

With the establishment of the Harpers Ferry National Historical Park in 1959—exactly one hundred years after the John Brown raid—the Federal government took possession of the Storer buildings. Park officials had the engine house moved from the campus to a small, grassy lot down near the junction of the rivers, across Shenandoah Street from the spot where it had stood a century before. Park rangers are fond of pointing out that the building is backwards.

Each year the Harpers Ferry park draws roughly a million visitors, and all but a tiny fraction of them stop in at the engine house. Often they are disappointed; the building seems much too small for the giant story it has to tell. Occasionally, people are seen holding pocket mirrors and looking over their shoulders with them, hoping no doubt, to catch a glimpse of John Brown's Fort as it looked on the day of the raid.

The engine house is not, by any means, the park's only attraction. Although tiny, only a few dozen acres, there is plenty to see. Besides the usual run of films and glassed-case exhibits, most of them having to do with the John Brown raid, there is the rock where Jefferson first hailed his famous view, Harper's stone house, the cemetery where Harper and many of the town's other heroes are buried, the Storer campus, and much more.

The more adventurous walk over the Potomac trestle, to see the ruins of the C & O canal and the ruins of the lockkeeper's house where the abolitionist raider John Cook lived and spied on the town. Following the demise of the canal in

1924, the keeper's house became a notorious saloon. Prohibition moonshiners are said to have kept a nearby water tower topped off with their illicit brew. Supposedly, B & O freight trains made frequent stops at the tower to fill a special tank car with a sloshing load of whiskey intended for thirsty customers in Baltimore and Washington.

John Cook was not the only Harpers Ferry spy. If a visitor asks enough people, someone will point out the house where a World War II German spy lived and kept count of the trains passing over the B & O tracks. As things often go in Harpers Ferry, the local experts do not always point to the same house when they tell the story of the Nazi spy.

"We shall proceed to the Ferry"

Practically every structure still standing in or around Harper's Ferry can lay claim to a fascinating past. Standing on a high ledge overlooking the Potomac is the Hilltop House, an old and gracious hotel still treating guests to its breathtaking views. The hotel was built early in this century by Thomas Lovett, a black entrepreneur who, with his family, operated it for nearly fifty years. Woodrow Wilson and other U.S. presidents are known to have enjoyed the Hilltop's hospitality.

Perhaps the presidents paused on the veranda and looked out across the river to the Maryland cliffs to see if they could decide whose face was etched in the stone there. Harpers Ferry folks once thought the face was that of George Washington. Later, the stone face altered its features and became first John Brown and then Abraham Lincoln. It is delightful to imagine that after studying the stones for more than seventy years, Joseph Barry finally saw his own face there.

By the 1950s, the old hotel, with its extraordinary view, had fallen on hard times, but its fortunes were destined to improve. In 1959, Baltimore lawyer Dixie Kilham saw the Hilltop and fell in love with it. Shoving his law degree in a drawer, he bought the place and became an innkeeper.

Perhaps no town in America can claim a history more vibrant, violent, or important than that of Harpers Ferry, shown here clinging to its blade of rock.
(Photo courtesy of **Bruce Roberts**)

Among Kilham's first guests was the actor George Mason on location in Harpers Ferry to play the role of John Brown in a made-for-television movie about the raid.

"Back then, the plumbing was not so good," said Kilham. "And one day Mason couldn't get any hot water out of the spigot for his bath." Kilham told two of his porters to take a large coffee urn full of hot water up to Mason's room. Unfortunately, they took the wrong urn and dumped a tub full of coffee into Mason's bath.

One night Mason and his crew went out across the Potomac to film an important scene by torchlight. John Brown was about to launch his raid on Harpers Ferry. Kilham brought along gallons of coffee—and bottles of whiskey—for the actors and crew.

"Everyone drank a lot of coffee and, frankly, a lot of whiskey." said Kilham. "They kept messing up the scene. Mason was supposed to jump up on the seat of a wagon and make a speech to his men. But a pair of mules were hitched to the wagon, and each time Mason jumped up there, the startled mules lurched forward and over he went. One time Mason fell all the way down into the C & O canal, and they had to redo his makeup and everything. Then, way into the night, they finally got the scene just right. It was one of those things you remember."

Kilham knew the television movie would capture only a little of the truth about John Brown. Historical truth is a shadowy thing, especially in Harpers Ferry, where opposing rivers of history come together with great violence. It can never be seen directly, only in reflection, as in a mirror or in a formation of stones on a cliff. Usually, when we look down into the murky waters of our past, the face we see is our own.

But that night on the movie set, Kilham thought he caught a fleeting glimpse of the true past. "Mason got up on the wagon, and this time the mules were still. He raised his arms and started to speak and this mysterious thing happened. He was no longer an actor. He was the real John

Brown and we were all standing there 100 years ago waiting for him to change the world."

And John Brown said: "Men, get on your arms. We shall proceed to the Ferry."

Index